KEEPING FAITH IN FUNDRAISING

Keeping Faith in Fundraising

Peter Harris and Rod Wilson

WILLIAM B. EERDMANS PUBLISHING COMPANY
GRAND RAPIDS, MICHIGAN

Wm. B. Eerdmans Publishing Co.
2140 Oak Industrial Drive NE, Grand Rapids, Michigan 49505
www.eerdmans.com

23 22 21 20 19 18 17   1 2 3 4 5 6 7

ISBN 978-0-8028-7462-7

Library of Congress Cataloging-in-Publication Data

Names: Harris, Peter, 1952-   author. | Wilson, Rod, author.
Title: Keeping faith in fundraising / Peter Harris and Rod Wilson.
Description: Grand Rapids, Michigan : William B. Eerdmans Publishing Company,
    2017. | Includes bibliographical references.
Identifiers: LCCN 2016035931 | ISBN 9780802874627 (pbk. : alk. paper)
Subjects: LCSH: Church fund raising. | Fund raisers (Persons)
Classification: LCC BV772.5 .H25 2017 | DDC 254/.8—dc23
    LC record available at https://lccn.loc.gov/2016035931

Scripture quotations are taken from the New International Version of the Bible
unless otherwise indicated.

Contents

Acknowledgments

I, Peter, would like to express my deep gratitude to so many I cannot name who have encouraged me on the long road toward fundraising faithfully. They include donors, critics, good listeners, and hard questioners. I also want to thank several of our potential donors who declined to give, but did so really well and helpfully.

It is good to be able to name a few A Rocha friends and colleagues who have been particular companions on the fundraising journey—but worrying also, as I am sure there are many others I should mention, but haven't. Please forgive me, as you know who you are! Write and complain and I owe you. But thank you, in no particular order, Bob and Margaret Pullan, Rachel Simonson, Barbara Mearns, David and Betty Payne, Annali Bamber-Jones, Mark Mariotti, Amy Owen, Sarah Walker, Sarah Young, Matthias Stiefel, Rebecca Irvin, Markku Kostamo, Arnaud Monnoyeur, Marcial and Paula Felgueiras, Colin Jackson, Tom Rowley, Ginny Vroblesky, Sir Ghillean and Lady Anne Prance, Chris Naylor, and David McKay. I am very grateful to each one of you as it seems I am unable to fundraise dispassionately, and you have all been very understanding!

Many others such as Mike O'Neill, Steve Beck, David Jones, Fred Smith, Brook Hazelton, Brent Fearon, Geoff Cowper, Stanley Martin, and Anne Habberton were generous with their sage advice as Miranda and I began navigating the reef-filled waters of North American fundraising and we are very appreciative. Any wrecks I left behind were from my own steering.

It is a shame not to be able to thank many of our donors by name—you lit lanterns on our path by your kindness as you patiently took time to understand A Rocha's vision and passions. The hard questions you put to us may have been painful at times, but they have helped us build a better organization and be clearer about what we were trying to do. So thank you. I cannot resist thanking some of the wealthier among you for some spectacular meals you have hosted, and for your invitation into worlds so different from our own.

Fundraising for an organization like A Rocha involves a lot of travel, and for most of our working years there were no funds for that. So we thank all the many friends who have lent rooms, sofas, floor-space, cars, and telephones in the old days, and office facilities in the new. Your tactful suggestions for how to recover from fundraising meetings that went badly, like distracting episodes of *The West Wing*, or time watching starling roosts at sunset, made a great difference and kept us going, as did the coffee. Un grand merci.

It has been a real privilege over the years to have learned from, and exchanged stories and reflections with, Rod Wilson. That he graciously agreed for us to write this together was a gift, and the process has taught me a great deal. I admire his searing honesty, grit, and tenacity in pursuing visions with deep humility and locked-tight efficiency. He is methodical where I am impulsive, and I dare to think we make a reasonable team. He and I both know that we owe our working sanity to the sane companionship of our wives in many aspects of the fundraising tasks as so many others, and Bev has brought gaiety and wisdom to many of our conversations. So thank you too for this partnership.

I thank our family, Jo, Esther, Jeremy, and Beth, who over the first twenty years of A Rocha's life bore the brunt of my frequent failure to raise the funds we needed, or at least thought we needed. Although it was a struggle to keep the show on the road at times, you never complained, and you made it all fun, even if the words *improvise* and *adventure* should never have acquired the sharp edges they occasionally showed. We admire you all for what you have made, in your own working lives, of fundraising, money and the lack of it, as you have embraced a needy world in some wonderfully creative ways.

Finally I want to say that the still point of the last forty years has always been Miranda. She has shared all that our choices implied with grace and deep courage and knows more than anyone what keeping faith in fundraising means too. As usual, the text of this book is far better for the editorial care she took with it. I know that care will extend to all that the coming years hold for us, and thank you that wherever it is, we will go there together.

*   *   *

I, Rod, want to express my gratitude to co-pilgrims at Christian Counselling Services, Tyndale College and Seminary, Hilltop Chapel, International Medical Service, Interest Ministries, Africa Inland Mission, Christian Higher Education in Canada, Forest Brook Community Church, Regent College, Capilano Christian Community, Association of Theological Schools, The Roundtable, A Rocha, and many other communities where I have learned much about what it means to have a vibrant ministry that requires financial support. It was in these contexts that I was given many examples of the relationship between money and mission and the inextricable link between what we do and how it is funded.

I am indebted to hundreds of donors (who for obvious reasons need to remain nameless) for their engagement, sacrifice, friendship, and obedience to God and the way all of that has contributed to my understanding of fundraising and God's work in the world.

It was from many of these people that I learned that giving is a gift and that often the wealthy are caricatured in ways that do not reflect the reality of how they actually live. But more than that, I have been struck by the generosity of those with little, who have learned what it means to live a Christ-centered life of sacrifice.

Christie Goode, Richard Thompson, Tim Boland, Karissa Hsueh, and Hilary Guth constitute the finest fundraising team I have worked with because they understood that fundraising was about so much more than raising funds. It was from this team of people that I learned much about the ethos of fundraising, the importance of blending programmatic efficiency with a deep faith in God, and the centrality of having a fundraising team that saw the raising of funds as a spiritual activity. In God's economy this team will receive their reward with standards that far surpass the amount of money they raised.

At various times and in different ways Bev Bandstra, Tim Boland, Uli Chi, Brent Fearon, Alan Gilman, Christie Goode, Greg Pennoyer, Larry Matthews, Mark Petersen, Phil Reilly, Peter Roebbelen, Gail Stevenson, and Richard Thompson helped me refine what I wanted to say in writing, though they bear no responsibility for the final product. While writing is often a solo endeavor, these individuals have particular insights into the world of fundraising and gave their time, energy, and effort in a sacrificial way.

Each of the staff members that Peter and I have worked with at Eerdmans has been encouraging, supportive, and responsive. In particular we want to acknowledge the engagement of Michael Thomson, Jenny Hoffman, Laura Bardolph Hubers, and Vicky Fanning, who served as caring midwives in the birth of this volume.

Miranda Harris, my friend, has been instrumental in the world of fundraising as it has applied to A Rocha and contributed much to this book through various conversations when the four of us were together as well as through her editorial eye. While my name is on the cover of the book along with Miranda's husband

Peter, her insights forged in the donor arena have added great value to my perspective and convictions.

My friend and fellow writer Peter Harris is one of the most passionate, thoughtful, visionary, and engaging people I know, and he brought all of that and much more to bear on our relationship, our many conversations about fundraising, and this book. We have argued that fundraising needs to be approached like every other area of the Christian life, and for me Peter is one of the best exemplars of how to live this kind of an integrated life under God.

Bev is my wife and friend, so has been with me on many fundraising trips and visits, lived with me through the joy of raising funds for many communities, experienced my inner angst and her own while trying to do this work well, and has continued through all of it with her characteristic commitment to prayer, faithfulness, friendship, and joy. She has often been my best fundraising consultant, my main conscience on whether I am living faithfully under God, and the person who has best embodied what it means to live the Christian life fully.

The triune God has shown me again, in one more area of the Christian life, that all my intent, planning, and activity have their place but only in the context of his providence, sovereignty, and will, and that all the good that happens in the world can be traced ultimately to his goodness. For many years I thought fundraising was distinct from other areas of my life with God, but I have learned, to my great surprise, that my own maturity in Christ has been facilitated by being a fundraiser. Who would have thought?

Introduction

On our very first meeting seventeen years ago we began talking about fundraising. For both of us it had been a major component of our working lives and as we talked we realized we had been on a considerable journey. That journey had been one that began in reluctance, and had continued in occasional exhilaration, frequent bafflement, almost constant frustration, and even emotional turmoil. Now, we realized, we were coming into a new season where we had both sensed a renewed calling to fundraising as ministry. Over the next ten years we continued to share stories and learning until we finally realized it was time to draw some of the threads together so we could understand better what we had lived through, and where we might be going in this very demanding part of our working lives. We had begun to realize that we were not alone in the complex set of reactions that the challenge of both fundraising and giving evokes in many people and so we were encouraged to write this book.

We wanted to examine the relationships that lie at the heart of fundraising which faithfully reflect the character of the triune God. We wanted to bring fundraising back where it belongs within normal Christian life and work, inspired by the Holy Spirit, modeled on Jesus, in conversation with our loving Father.

We wanted to establish some solid biblical foundations for what is almost intrinsically and intentionally a risky enterprise, rather like the farming and fishing that Scripture offers as model activities for all growth that is begun, continues, and ends in faith. So what follows is the fruit of our own learning, and conversations with literally hundreds of both donors and fundraisers.

Rod begins with a story:

It was a donor meeting in a restaurant, and I was faced with the familiar challenge of listening wisely to the donor and speaking with integrity about our college's vision. My wife Bev was beside me at the small round table as she often was at these meetings, and as always I was grateful for her prayerful spirit and engaging sense of humor. Across from us was someone we had known for a long time. Warm and winsome and sharp as a tack, she had broad interests and spoke with a wide knowledge of many subjects. She had been widowed a few years earlier and had never given to our community out of her own funds, but our college had been the recipient of a generous gift for a building campaign that came from their family foundation. Our recent meetings had been out of friendship with her, and not interest in her family's philanthropy, as it would not have been appropriate to talk to her about funds when she was in the middle of a grief journey.

Many months before that particular lunch, I had mentioned to her that the college wanted to put in place an endowed chair in Christianity and the arts. While so much of the Christian world seemed to work around a large chasm between these two areas, our institution saw the arts and the Christian faith as integrated and recognized that both find their source in the true Creator. As she was a patron of the arts, this had resonated strongly with her existing interests, and I had been able to outline the financial realities of such an undertaking. An endowed chair would require an investment of $3 million, which would be put in our foundation, and the interest that accrued in subsequent years would be used to cover a number of facets of the arts at the school. She was not the only one who had heard the case; I had spoken with many people but after a few years had raised only $1.7 million of the $3 million target.

It is clearly a "first world problem" when you are discouraged that "only" $1.7 million has been given, but raising it was my task and I cannot deny that it was how I felt at the time. When you set a philanthropic target, believe it is for a good cause, and ask people to contribute, you hope that you will meet the goal, but I was "only" a little over halfway. And to compound the problem I was running out of people to talk to and was having trouble generating another list. So while extremely thankful to those who had got us to $1.7 million, I had begun to strategize about how to have the chair with less money invested. It was quite straightforward actually. If we did this or that, then maybe we could move in this direction or that one. The joys of human initiative and diligence!

My preparation for the lunch included self-statements along the lines of "she has not said anything about the endowed chair in spite of previous communications, so more than likely her silence means no, and it would be better to steer clear of that subject today, and maybe follow up the meeting with an indirect 'so have you thought any more about the endowed chair?' but maybe even that would be unwise." Fundraisers may know that internal bind. You are trying to read the cues, and listen to the messages and the sounds of silence; and so you pay attention, listen well, and are respectful. So I went into the meeting discouraged, thinking that this was simply the prelude to another meeting, which would have to be rescheduled with all the complications that entails. There was also some frustration as I realized again that many are the preludes in the life of a fundraiser!

After an extended time of catching up on our lives I was taken aback when the following question came from the other side of the round table: "Can you tell me more about where things are with that chair you were hoping to establish in Christianity and the arts?" Fundraisers may be told that they should not be surprised by anything, and much less show it, but I think I came close to falling off my chair. She was not supposed to ask this question, but I was able to get out a few sentences to the effect that I was encouraged that some funding had come in and things were moving along. I also knew that fundraisers were supposed to be positive, so I dug deep and did my best.

"How much have you raised?" she enquired.

"1.7 of the 3 million," I replied.

"That is really interesting because I went to see my financial advisor last week and told him that I was going to give you $1.3 million when you came to visit me today."

I have done enough fundraising and read enough books to know that my next line should have been eloquent and bathed in gratitude, but I could not get any words out. I was simply too emotional, which for some may be unprofessional, inappropriate, and certainly not in step with the dignity of asking for money, but it was not a choice! It was clear that Bev and our donor friend across the table were similarly moved. You get the picture? Two adults with an older adult in a nice restaurant, all deeply affected by their conversation. I have often wondered since that day how others in the restaurant saw this interchange. Was it a couple telling a close friend that they are getting a divorce? Was it an older person indicating that she has terminal cancer? Was this the first meal after a husband and father died? But it was none of these. It was an incredibly specific moment in a fundraising relationship where a particular financial need was met with inexplicable precision by a prayerful donor. It was an event that could not be accounted for by any natural, observable, measureable means, nor could it be replicated by the utilization of a foolproof technique, or understood as a reflection of the brilliance of the fundraiser.

In many ways what happened round that table and my attempts to understand it, taken together with our shared wrestling with a long series of philanthropic experiences, are what raised many of the questions that led us to write this book. If we call ourselves Christian fundraisers, is this story normative in the sense that this is how things should happen all the time? Was it in the realm of the miraculous and so should we expect encounters like that only infrequently while our "normal" ways of fundraising dominate the rest of the time? Was it simply coincidental and there was no clearly divine aspect to the lunchtime interchange? Are there principles embedded in this story that need to be teased out and understood as we establish some biblical, theological, and spiritual ground for understanding fundraising?

*   *   *

As we wrote this book it became apparent to me (Peter) that we were working across at least five fault lines or great divides, all of which are illustrated in this story. The first one emerged as we fought our way across our own cultural fault lines to write a book that works for us both, and so hopefully for others in equally different and varied contexts. Rod's fundraising meal took place in a Canadian context, and we are both aware that there are major differences between the Canadian and British cultures that we come from. The way some Canadians are able to talk of money is quite different from the discretion that most British people prefer, and I would imagine the story itself could generate many diverse cultural reactions. A good friend of mine worked as personal assistant for many years to one of the most entrepreneurial Christian leaders of his generation. The man he worked for had written hundreds of fundraising letters, all typed by my friend, but when I told him that I was writing a book on fundraising he simply said, "O dear . . . (long distasteful pause), why?" Talk of money, or fundraising, is inevitably in bad taste in some circles.

Given that fundraising itself is conducted very differently all around the world, I wonder whether Rod's opening story reflects both unique cultural features and some common facets that would be true anywhere. Would donors in the UK or China, for instance, be as transparent as this woman, or would fundraisers in other countries respond with tears to such a large and exact gift? We have both raised funds in many countries and seen striking cultural differences between them, but we have become very aware that much of the potential and many of the problems of contemporary fundraising as practiced by Christians seem common to all.

Secondly, and more seriously than the cultural divide we faced, we realized that for each of us, the topic of fundraising itself was haunted by the space that can open up between the donor who has means on one side of the relationship, and the person or organization who has needs on the other. This power imbalance frequently seems to be the unspoken and unwelcome guest in any conversation, and in different ways it affects people on both sides. While Rod's experience of weakness and inadequacy was met with the donor's relinquishing of financial power and control, we recognize, sadly, that this may be unusual in most of our fundraising meetings.

The power imbalance has caused us some grief over the years, and we know we are not alone. As we interviewed donors and fundraisers to calibrate our conclusions for this book, we heard stories that were freighted with frustration and even pain. So we want to look hard at power and vulnerability by looking at these questions that lie at the very heart of the gospel. It may be that we can make progress by recovering our confidence that fundraising itself can be redeemed so it can do biblical justice to both strength and weakness, however we perceive them.

Our third divide also made itself felt in the encounter that Rod has related above, and it is the gap that constantly threatens to open up between pragmatism and principle. "Whatever works" would seem to be the guiding rule for much of the fundraising that we have come across in a number of Christian subcultures. Or perhaps that should be sub-Christian cultures. Either way, and even more unfortunately, we have heard the phrase "in the real world" as a frequent framing for Christian talk and behavior about money. It is as if financial considerations mean that belief or trust in God becomes impractical. We have seen this pragmatism manifesting itself in suspect arguments, opaque accounting, certainty that donors must respond as the social sciences predict they will, reliance on technique, and the unspoken assumption that bigger is going to be better for any Christian organization. As we have looked honestly at our experience in fundraising, punctuated as it has been by a number of episodes such as the one Rod has recounted, we find it hard to offer any pragmatic lessons as they are constantly subverted by the inexplicable and apparently grace-filled surprises. But we do think there are some principles that we have learned, and we hope to explain them as best we can in the pages that follow.

We assume that those who trust in God rather than putting their faith in mere expertise or pragmatism want their fundraising to be rooted in the appropriate soil. However, we have both been troubled by how to work out of a redeemed approach to fundraising that focuses on faith and vision without relying unduly on competence or technique.

A fourth and serious divide is between the way money is earned and how it is given. On the occasion of the major gift, Rod did not know the source, either at the time or subsequently. He knew the donor well and trusted her and that was the compass he used. However, we believe that for a Christian it is vitally important that the funds are accumulated in a way that is coherent with how and to whom they are given. Many foundations, and even churches, currently support all kinds of important causes. But surprisingly often they are investing their money in companies and commercial enterprises that are adding to the very ills in society, and abuses of creation, that their own foundation exists to heal or combat, and that the churches lament. A minimal screening that simply avoids the more obvious "sins" of arms, tobacco, and pornography, in order to take a common "ethical" approach, proves very little in our complex and fragmented times. In particular, the negative impact on creation of much conventional investing—which gives financial oxygen to activities that accelerate biodiversity loss and climate change for example—is far more devastating than is generally realized. Added to all this, many never consider the lost opportunity for truly virtuous impact investing, which is taking up a rapidly growing share of the heavy lifting in the areas of social development and poverty relief, thereby releasing more classical charitable funds for work that cannot find a business model in commercial sustainability.

The cause for that lack of reflection on how our money is earned probably lies in the deepest divide of all—between what we believe and what we do. This dualism needs challenging not only because it is far from a biblical view of life, but also because its consequences are disabling. In particular, few areas of Christian thought and practice are as deeply affected by dualism as those where money enters into the picture.

It is because we believe that dualism is our most persistent and deeply rooted difficulty that we suspect the most important part of the book is an attempt to rethink fundraising within its true biblical framework. We recognize as we do so that again we must work across another divide: the relevant biblical texts are rooted in the Middle East and in quite different economic eras. But the serious work of transposition and understanding is well worth the effort as it lifts us out of the unconscious and often unintentional comfort we find in our current cultures with all their quiet, even well-mannered, hostility to Christian thought.

So we want to consider the experience of fundraising within the relationships that lie at its heart—with God, creation, and with ourselves as creative and vulnerable people made in the image of the Trinity. We have come to believe that it is a grave mistake to think of fundraising as merely about finding money. When we do, we risk causing ourselves, our donors, and creation all kinds of damage. We are convinced that fundraising is fundamentally a question of finding support for causes we care about in a way that honors those core relationships, and in conversation with Christ, and we hope we can persuade you!

*   *   *

We have found it necessary to lay down many inherited ideas about money and fundraising, and indeed the normal Christian life. They have reached us both from the wider culture and from the Christian subculture that we encountered in many parts of the world and in different contexts of wealth and poverty. We are attempting to return fundraising, and our attitudes to money and therefore power, to the heart of our faith where they all belong. We have told some stories, appropriately anonymized, shared some hard lessons learned, and examined some of the core themes that we have detected within what we believe to be a godly calling to raise funds.

Much of what we have written is the outcome not only of our friendship and conversations about philanthropy over many years but also of our work in fundraising for different churches and organizations, our consulting with other individuals and institutions, and our personal reflections on that work. We have no sense that we are outstanding fundraisers, setting a bar for others to reach, and writing a book with the definitive word on this topic. We write as co-pilgrims with others who have sought to raise funds. We have struggled as fundraisers and look back to a number of situations wishing the outcomes had been different, the relationships stronger, and our trust in God deeper. But we have also seen glimpses of God working, usually in spite of us, not because of us, and we have been grateful that from time to time we have glimpsed such remarkable grace in events for which no other explanation seems possible. So we write on this topic with an acute sense of dependence on God. Although we have both worked to raise funds somewhat in the public eye with its usual accolades and criticisms, this book is not an attempt to claim success or excuse failure. Like every other aspect of the Christian life, we have sought to do our philanthropic work faithfully by living to an audience of One, and we believe that the ultimate and final assessment of what we or others might imagine to be successes and failures has yet to occur. So we expect a lot of surprises.

The book is divided into three sections—starting with Scripture, focusing on themes, and offering our stories. The biblical section provides a detailed analysis of 2 Corinthians chapters 8 and 9, an ancient text that provides wise instruction and correction for the contemporary world of fundraising. Coming out of these two chapters, the thematic section expands on seven themes and their centrality in understanding the giving and receiving of money—integration, people, work, success, need, method, and money. The final section is biographical in the sense that we both describe our experiences, questions, confusion, suggestions, and wonder as we have sought to raise funds for many causes.

We have started with the biblical material because of our belief that the sacred text is foundational for Christian fundraising. We recognize, however, that some readers will want to start with the biographical section because it appears more interesting, is easier to understand, and does not require any biblical expertise. Others will want to start with the seven-part thematic section because they enjoy reflecting on principles and find that kind of material to be a springboard for their own ideas. We recognize that some may find the biblical section unfamiliar territory and maybe even too intense, but we hope that with time it will repay the effort as there are amazing and deeply practical truths to be found in these essential texts.

It is our hope and prayer that this volume will:

- deepen our awareness that all aspects of any work in the kingdom of God, including fundraising, need to take their direction from the King of that kingdom;

- generate more conversation, writing, and reflection on what it means to be not just a fundraiser but a truly Christian fundraiser;
- provoke a fresh look at the current state of Christian fundraising;
- encourage individuals, organizations, and churches that raise funds;
- aid departments, boards, and fundraising teams that want to assess their fundraising culture; and
- stimulate donors to reflect on what it is like for those who ask them for money.

It is our prayer that fundraising, this critical and important element of Christian work, can be lifted out of its shadowy corner and into a new and brighter place that more closely reflects what we believe about the God who is our creator and provider.

STARTING WITH SCRIPTURE

CHAPTER 1

Biblical Grounding

It is inconceivable to write a book on philanthropy from a Christian perspective without starting with the Bible. So slowly read 2 Corinthians 8 and 9 with expectancy and curiosity.

8 And now, brothers and sisters, we want you to know about the grace that God has given the Macedonian churches. ²In the midst of a very severe trial, their overflowing joy and their extreme poverty welled up in rich generosity. ³For I testify that they gave as much as they were able, and even beyond their ability. Entirely on their own, ⁴they urgently pleaded with us for the privilege of sharing in this service to the Lord's people. ⁵And they exceeded our expectations: They gave themselves first of all to the Lord, and then by the will of God also to us. ⁶So we urged Titus, just as he had earlier made a beginning, to bring also to completion this act of grace on your part. ⁷But since you excel in everything—in faith, in speech, in knowledge, in complete earnestness and in the love we have kindled in you—see that you also excel in this grace of giving.

⁸I am not commanding you, but I want to test the sincerity of your love by comparing it with the earnestness of others. ⁹For you know the grace of our Lord Jesus Christ, that though he was

rich, yet for your sake he became poor, so that you through his poverty might become rich.

[10]And here is my judgment about what is best for you in this matter. Last year you were the first not only to give but also to have the desire to do so. [11]Now finish the work, so that your eager willingness to do it may be matched by your completion of it, according to your means. [12]For if the willingness is there, the gift is acceptable according to what one has, not according to what one does not have.

[13]Our desire is not that others might be relieved while you are hard pressed, but that there might be equality. [14]At the present time your plenty will supply what they need, so that in turn their plenty will supply what you need. The goal is equality, [15]as it is written: "The one who gathered much did not have too much, and the one who gathered little did not have too little."

[16]Thanks be to God, who put into the heart of Titus the same concern I have for you. [17]For Titus not only welcomed our appeal, but he is coming to you with much enthusiasm and on his own initiative. [18]And we are sending along with him the brother who is praised by all the churches for his service to the gospel. [19]What is more, he was chosen by the churches to accompany us as we carry the offering, which we administer in order to honor the Lord himself and to show our eagerness to help. [20]We want to avoid any criticism of the way we administer this liberal gift. [21]For we are taking pains to do what is right, not only in the eyes of the Lord but also in the eyes of man.

[22]In addition, we are sending with them our brother who has often proved to us in many ways that he is zealous, and now even more so because of his great confidence in you. [23]As for Titus, he is my partner and co-worker among you; as for our brothers, they are representatives of the churches and an honor to Christ. [24]Therefore show these men the proof of your love and the reason for our pride in you, so that the churches can see it.

9 There is no need for me to write to you about this service to the Lord's people. [2]For I know your eagerness to help, and I

have been boasting about it to the Macedonians, telling them that since last year you in Achaia were ready to give; and your enthusiasm has stirred most of them to action. ³But I am sending the brothers in order that our boasting about you in this matter should not prove hollow, but that you may be ready, as I said you would be. ⁴For if any Macedonians come with me and find you unprepared, we—not to say anything about you—would be ashamed of having been so confident. ⁵So I thought it necessary to urge the brothers to visit you in advance and finish the arrangements for the generous gift you had promised. Then it will be ready as a generous gift, not as one grudgingly given.

⁶Remember this: Whoever sows sparingly will also reap sparingly, and whoever sows generously will also reap generously. ⁷Each of you should give what you have decided in your heart to give, not reluctantly or under compulsion, for God loves a cheerful giver. ⁸And God is able to bless you abundantly, so that in all things at all times, having all that you need, you will abound in every good work. ⁹As it is written:

"They have freely scattered their gifts to the poor;
their righteousness endures forever."

¹⁰Now he who supplies seed to the sower and bread for food will also supply and increase your store of seed and will enlarge the harvest of your righteousness. ¹¹You will be enriched in every way so that you can be generous on every occasion, and through us your generosity will result in thanksgiving to God.

¹²This service that you perform is not only supplying the needs of the Lord's people but is also overflowing in many expressions of thanks to God. ¹³Because of the service by which you have proved yourselves, others will praise God for the obedience that accompanies your confession of the gospel of Christ, and for your generosity in sharing with them and with everyone else. ¹⁴And in their prayers for you their hearts will go out to you, because of the surpassing grace God has given you. ¹⁵Thanks be to God for his indescribable gift!

CHAPTER 2

Biblical Reflections

Warning! We are very aware that many fundraisers, including those who would self-identify as Christians, may not be particularly interested in working through two chapters from the Bible. Their daily struggle is how to raise funds, and what they really want are well-defined techniques that will help them produce the money that is being required by their organization. The Bible? Theology? These are for the academy, the seminary, the graduate school where people have the leisure to grapple with these lofty matters. And what, after all, does the ancient Bible have to do with fundraising in the twenty-first century? Can it really help anyone in the daily reality of working life?

We invite those who are asking such questions to give the Bible a chance. Let it speak and explain itself. Pray that your consideration of the text might turn on the lights, open the curtains, and make the way clearer. We both believe that there are riches for fundraisers to find in these verses, but it will require patience and commitment to move slowly through the material before jumping to themes that appear more interesting, or biographies that seem more appealing.

For those who believe that fundraising is a "dirty business," removed from anything spiritual or Christian and lacking in virtue and nobility, 2 Corinthians 8 and 9 are arresting. Following chapters 1–7, which are biographical in nature and provide a defense of Paul's apostolic ministry and his experience with hardships, and preceding chapters 10–13, which focus on Paul's strength in weakness as support for his apostolic authority, these two chapters provide a detailed analysis of fundraising. Based on the financial need of the Jewish believers in Jerusalem and the example of the Macedonian Christians who gave generously, Paul solicits funds from the Corinthians with a direct and overt appeal, and he even says he will feel ashamed if they fail to fulfill their promise.

If we read Scripture as exclusively prescriptive, we could squeeze these two chapters into a list of "how-to's" and conclude that all fundraising must be done through the church, that it can only focus on the poor, that three people must always collect the offering, and that one Christian community needs to be held up as both the model and the motivator for other communities to give generously. Such an approach takes the narrative out of its historical context and presupposes that all the cultural dynamics in the early church can easily be transposed into the contemporary setting. On the other hand, to read 2 Corinthians 8 and 9 as purely descriptive runs the risk of placing the narrative solely in its own context and ignores any principles that might be applicable to our own fundraising efforts.

As we have reflected on this text, seven themes have emerged—integration, people, work, success, need, method, and money. These themes have not only helped us understand the nature of Christian fundraising but also strengthened our belief that they are central to how we actually do philanthropic work.

1. Integration

While a nonintegrated perspective would separate the material from the spiritual, the secular from the sacred, and money from worship, the two Corinthian letters do not make these kinds of distinctions. After significant teaching addressing the Corinthians' theological, moral, ethical, and worship irregularities, the first epistle to the church at Corinth ends with a command to collect money on the first day of the week, including instructions on saving money for this purpose, making decisions about the appropriate amount in light of one's income, and giving particular direction as to where the money should go (1 Cor. 16:1-4). Not surprisingly, Paul revives the topic of giving in the second letter, showing again how his careful treatment of theology necessarily leads to a discussion of money.

Paul's concern for the churches is reflected throughout his epistles, but it is not confined to the nonmaterial areas of life. Jewish Christians in Jerusalem were poor largely because of famines (Acts 11:27-30) but also because they experienced economic and social disadvantages due to their allegiance to Jesus of Nazareth and because they were subject to both Jewish and Roman taxation systems. The apostle's response to their plight was rooted in his early call to minister to the Gentiles. While God directed Peter, James, and John to serve the Jews primarily, they gave their blessing to Paul in his work with the Gentiles, but reminded him that he should remember the poor (Gal. 2:6-10). His commitment, however, was not simply because he wanted to provide philanthropic support for a particular religious and ethnic group; it was also because such support would show Gentile churches like the one in Corinth that they were part of the same family as the Jewish believers in Jerusalem, and those who received the gift would realize that the uncircumcised Gentile followers of Jesus were concerned for their welfare. For Paul, the Gentiles owed their gift to the Jewish believers since they had the privilege of sharing in the spiritual blessings that had originally come to the Jews (Rom. 15:27). On the surface Paul's discussion about money may seem earthy or nonspiritual, but at the core it reflects his theological convictions that "all nations might believe and obey" Jesus (Rom.

16:26) and that in Christ the wall of hostility between Jew and Gentile has been broken down (Eph. 2:11-22). This unity must find expression even in the basic issue of money.

Paul's first letter to the church at Corinth focused on problems, and it is clear that the members were pained and grieved by what he said (2 Cor. 2:1-11). In the second letter he senses that his relationship with them has improved, his apostolic authority is intact in their eyes, and he takes pride in their growth. Titus is the key messenger in this process (2 Cor. 7:13-16), partly because of his strong connection with Paul but also because he has spent time with the Corinthian church and has inside information. When a leader confronts a community about its theological shortcomings, it is inevitable that there will be relational tension, but Paul is now on better terms with the church. Titus shares a connection and appreciation with both the apostle and the Corinthians, and the stage is set for Paul to make a financial request.

Apart from these broader contextual issues that show how Paul integrates his theology and practice, it is significant that the Greek word *charis* appears ten different times in these two chapters that focus on fundraising. Normally translated as "grace," this word is central to our understanding of the gospel, and here it is linked with God providing financial resources for us to give (2 Cor. 8:1; 9:8, 14), divine generosity embedded in Jesus Christ (8:9), the privilege of participating in giving (8:4), the offering itself (8:6, 19), the act of giving financially (8:7), and an expression of thanks to God (8:16; 9:15). In 2 Corinthians 8 and 9, grace is not a theological construct that is allocated to some higher spiritual plane, but rather something that gives philanthropy its very character.

Furthermore, it is these chapters on financial giving that contain two of the clearest Christological declarations in the entire Bible. In the first (2 Cor. 8:9), Jesus is described as having been rich and becoming poor, and this economic distinction rooted in grace is used as a model for how the Corinthians should understand the sacrifice of the Macedonians. In his doxological conclusion or worship hymn at the end of the entire argument, Paul expresses his thanks to God for the gift of Christ that is beyond verbal description but is nevertheless an example for generosity and sacrificial giving (2 Cor. 9:15). While it is not uncommon to lift both of these passages out of their context to make theological statements about who Christ is, it is striking that they form part of an integrated fabric that is about how we understand money and how we engage in its faithful stewardship.

If God is in all and over all, we should not be surprised that he is omnipresent in these two chapters. Principles about fundraising, details about the collection, and injunctions on methods are interspersed easily and integrated naturally with God's provision (2 Cor. 8:1), the Lord's people (8:4; 9:1, 12), obedience to the Lord (8:5), will of God (8:5), grace of our Lord Jesus Christ (8:9), thanks to God (8:16; 9:15), honoring the Lord (8:19), eyes of the Lord (8:21), honor to Christ (8:23), God loving (9:7), God blessing (9:8), God supplying (9:10), thanksgiving to God (9:11), praise to God (9:12), gospel of Christ (9:13), and grace of God (9:14). What we do with our money and how we understand God and his work in the world are seamlessly woven together.

2. People

One might expect that thirty-nine verses on fundraising would focus on money and that people would be described only as instrumental agents to arrive at a financial goal. However, a careful reading of the text reveals that this is not the case, as Paul pulls together reflections on a wide series of issues from motivation, sharing, administration, and donor benefits to consideration of a deep understanding of people as being part of a community.

Throughout Paul's ministry, his concern for the interdependence of believers, regardless of linguistic, ethnic, racial, gender, and religious barriers, is obvious (Rom. 12:13; 13:8; 1 Cor. 12:25–

26; Gal. 3:28, 29; 6:10). People were not isolated individuals but members of a body, a community, a family that transcended their unique qualities, gifts, and traits and identified them as part of something substantial and more significant. While Paul had his own clear call to serve the Gentiles in spite of being raised in Judaism and zealously persecuting Christians, he recognized that Peter had a similar call to serve the Jews (Gal. 1:11–2:21), and he was continually aware of the risk to the people of God if Jews and Gentiles were divided (Acts 15). Being part of a people who belonged to Christ was the central truth whether you were a Jew or a Gentile (Gal. 3:29).

This understanding of Christian community becomes a key argument when Paul asks the Corinthians to give. Paul describes the churches in Philippi and Thessalonica, located in the Roman province of Macedonia, as those who in spite of difficulties and poverty experienced joy in giving to the point of pleading with the apostle to let them give (2 Cor. 8:1–5). No donation figure is cited, and no details of the process they utilized are outlined. They are simply generous Gentile people, concerned for their Jewish brothers and sisters who are part of the whole family.

Central to the motivation of the Macedonians is the sense of privilege in sharing in this contribution of funds for the Jewish believers. To the Greek listener, the use of the term *koinonia* for sharing (2 Cor. 8:4) would be rich with meaning. It meant that they were not simply providing others with money from a distance but sharing fellowship and connection. The oneness of the body was enhanced and protected when the Macedonian churches were able to share with the Corinthians as co-donors to the project, but it also linked them with their brothers and sisters, the recipients of the gift in Jerusalem. For Paul, fundraising is not simply a transfer of funds but a personal and relational exchange that links donors both with each other and with recipients and thus manifests the interconnectedness of the people of God. In this context it is also significant that Paul understands that the gift of the Macedonians is to be given first to the Lord but then also to him (8:5). Again, the personal nature of the offering cannot be missed. God is the recipient of the sacrificial contribution, but Paul's relational role is not minimized.

Highly spiritualized approaches to fundraising may assume that careful attention to the administrative components of this work reveals a lack of virtue; however, Paul spends the last nine verses of 2 Corinthians 8 dealing with the mechanics of the gift, even though his emphasis is personal rather than technical (8:16-24). Titus is presented not as just an impersonal channel but as a person who is known both to Paul and to the Corinthians, and as someone who has initiative and enthusiasm. As Paul's partner and fellow worker he can be trusted to represent the churches and bring honor to Christ. Two other brothers are part of the administrative process, and like Titus these nameless individuals are known for their character and credibility and can be trusted with the conveyance of the large gift. Paul often found his integrity questioned (2:17; 11:7-11; 12:14-18) even in financial matters, so he took pains to do what was right in front of people and God (8:21) by selecting trustworthy people for the administrative work that was an inevitable part of the fundraising.

There are multiple benefits in providing funds, including the obvious one of meeting the financial needs of the Jewish believers in Jerusalem, but Paul reminds the Corinthians that what happens in them, and to them, may be the most important component of their sacrificial giving. In giving generously they will reap generously (2 Cor. 9:6), experience God's provision and abound in every good work (9:8), have an enlarged harvest of righteousness (9:10), experience riches for the purpose of greater generosity (9:11), precipitate the expression of gratitude to God by others (9:12-13), and experience the prayers and the heartfelt warmth of other Christians who are thankful for the manifestation of God's grace in their lives. Paul's concern for persons in community continues to take precedence, and any reflections on finances fit within that relational paradigm.

3. Work

At the beginning of each of Paul's letters, including 2 Corinthians, there is a humble self-reference that outlines how he understands the nature of his work. These important preludes help his hearers to recognize that he is not encouraging, rebuking, and instructing on a purely personal basis but rather that his writings are built on a substantive foundation. So, whether he refers to himself as a servant of Christ Jesus (Rom. 1:1; Phil. 1:1; Titus 1:1) or refers to his calling as an apostle (Rom. 1:1; 1 Cor. 1:1; 2 Cor. 1:1; Gal. 1:1; Eph. 1:1; Col. 1:1; 1 Tim. 1:1; 2 Tim. 1:1; Titus 1:1), he acknowledges both to others and to himself that he has not earned these designations, nor is he sent from people or by people (Gal. 1:1), but his apostolic authority originates in the will of God (1 Cor. 1:1; 2 Cor. 1:1; Eph. 1:1; 2 Tim. 1:1), in God's command (1 Tim. 1:1), and is linked with the promise of life that is in Christ Jesus (2 Tim. 1:2). As a result, all the fundraising material in 2 Corinthians 8 and 9 flows out of God-given authority. More significantly, we can understand that Paul as fundraiser sees himself doing God's work, and, just like his early readers, we can learn to value it no less than his work as a pastor, teacher, evangelist, or writer.

Not surprisingly, the nameless brother mentioned in 2 Corinthians 8:18-19, who is going to accompany Titus to Corinth to ensure they make good on their financial commitment, is described as someone not only with a good reputation among various churches but also as a person who is praised for his service to the gospel (2 Cor. 8:18). He is not simply a traveling companion, nor is he restricting his contribution to the technical administration of their task; rather, he is doing gospel work by, in this case, fundraising. The good news of Jesus Christ is not only at the heart of evangelism but also has a bearing on the collection of funds. When representatives of God and his churches engage in this kind of gospel work it should inevitably lead to eagerness to help, and in so doing such people honor the Lord (2 Cor. 8:19, 23).

But it is not only Paul the fundraiser and the nameless brothers who are engaging in work that is inextricably linked with God. The donors are also understood to be part of gospel work. Paul presupposes that those who have confessed the gospel of Christ will act in obedience by giving financially (2 Cor. 9:13). The Corinthians are reminded that if they do give, others will praise God, not simply because of the funds they provide but because their generosity has precipitated thanksgiving for the grace of God that is at work in their lives as the gospel penetrates more deeply.

When the work of fundraising is framed this way, we do not understand the recipients of the gift as needy people who are pleading for more money. Paul is careful to describe the Jewish believers in Jerusalem with theological language that invites the donors to see them not as distant and removed but as brothers and sisters. We do not know the details of the particular needs, but the Corinthians know that they are the Lord's people. On three different occasions (2 Cor. 8:4; 9:1, 12), Paul uses this phrase to capture the nature of the service that is being provided, a subtle reminder to the potential donors that they are not just giving to a project or to people, but are reaching out to those who belong to and are cherished by the Lord. They are his people. Within the cultural context of Jewish-Gentile tensions, such a phrase would remind the Gentile Corinthians that the recipients of their gift belong to the same Lord.

Given the centrality of the gospel in understanding the work of fundraising, it follows logically that Paul would speak directly about the gift of Jesus Christ. As Paul explains the earnest spirit that characterizes the giving of the Macedonians, he reminds the Corinthians that such giving is best exemplified by the Lord Jesus Christ (2 Cor. 8:9). The Macedonians were in challenging circumstances and in poverty, but in spite of both obstacles they gave with rich generosity (8:2). In other words, their experience of poverty did not get in the way of generosity. Jesus, quite apart from his economic circumstances here on earth, had unlimited preexistence with the Father and unparalleled heavenly glory in the triune God, but he chose not only to leave those riches but to come to earth, to live as a servant in human form, and to choose death, even death on a cross. What a stunning example of a road to poverty that illustrates something as earthy as fundraising (Phil. 2:5-11)!

The Philippian letter speaks to this profound Christological truth because it is vital that the body functions well in all its relationships (Phil. 2:1-4), but Paul uses reflections on Christ's descent into poverty as a way to motivate the Corinthians to give. Most of us would probably not use the poverty of one group of people to motivate another group to give. And we definitely would not speak about the remarkable descent of Christ as a way to cultivate pledge fulfillment. But for the apostle the question was clear. If the poor Macedonians could give generously, and Jesus living in heavenly riches could give that up for poverty, what was the problem with the Corinthians fulfilling their commitment to give? Again, the work of fundraising is not devoid of theological content nor removed from spirituality; the apostle takes great truths about Jesus's incarnation, along with earthly examples from the generosity of the Macedonians, to inspire the Corinthians.

While Paul links the sacrificial giving of the Son with choices that he made (2 Cor. 8:9), the final verse of this thirty-nine-verse Corinthian masterpiece expresses thanks to the Father for the gift he has provided, the gift of the Lord Jesus Christ, a gift that is beyond description in its depth and mystery (9:15). Again, such language is gospel centered, but it is not focused on conversion or personal evangelism. Those who understand the generosity of God's giving will recognize that the work of fundraising is actually rooted in the work of Jesus.

4. Success

Once we have read these two chapters that are bathed in grace, gift, generosity, and gratitude, the question of whether the fundraising was successful seems odd. If these theologically rich terms, rooted in the character of God, lie at the heart of Paul's fundraising appeal, can it be appropriate to determine his success or failure on simply financial terms? Yet even at that basic level the biblical record can give us some idea of whether it came up to that kind of mark.

The date of the writing of 2 Corinthians is debated in scholarly circles, but we do know from the book itself that Paul intended to visit Corinth for a third time (2 Cor. 12:14; 13:1), and according to the book of Acts (20:2-3) he went there for three months during which he wrote his letter to the Romans. At the end of that epistle he indicates that he is about to make a trip to Jerusalem to bring a contribution to the poor believers there, a contribution that comes from other believers in the region of Achaia where Corinth is located, as well as Macedonia (Rom. 15:25-26). If we assume, as many do, that Paul completed the book of Romans about five months after the completion of 2 Corinthians, it would appear that during this window his fundraising efforts were successful, even though we have no idea about the amount of money that was involved or the impact that it had.

However, the two chapters provide other metrics of success that mostly revolve around Paul's comparison of the giving of the Macedonians and the Corinthians. The former, in spite of their poverty, gave as much as they were able and even went on giving beyond their ability. They pleaded for the privilege of giving, they gave to the Lord and to Paul, and their gift was acceptable (2 Cor. 8:2-5, 12). In contrast, the Corinthians were not excelling in their giving. They were gifted in faith, speech, earnestness, and love, yet they were not demonstrating sincerity in their love, for even though they had pledged, their pledge fulfillment was sorely lacking (8:7-8, 11). While the churches in these two different geographical areas approached their fundraising in very distinct ways, Paul seems most concerned about the gap between intention and action.

Apparently Paul is not preoccupied with having a particular amount of money from the Macedonians and a different amount from the Corinthians. He is not using a financial metric with Macedonian churches as leverage to generate a particular amount among the Corinthians, as if this were a matching gift project. Paul seems to care more that their talk about giving had not produced much fruit even though they had made some contributions in the last year (2 Cor. 8:10). In that particular culture considerable emphasis was placed on intent, both in the criminal arena and in charitable service. A criminal act was less serious if it was done without intent, just as personal generosity only had virtue if the intent was there. By that particular standard, the Corinthians were unsuccessful. Because of this failure, Paul calls them to complete what they started (8:6), finish the work (8:11), match their willingness with completion (8:11), be ready to do what they said they would do (9:3), and finish what they had promised (9:5).

While Paul's apostolic ministry was often under scrutiny and criticism, he did everything he could to avoid discrediting his unique position as one empowered by God to reach the Gentiles (1 Cor. 9:12; 2 Cor. 4:2; 6:3). He risked failure in the eyes of others in all aspects of his ministry, and fundraising was no different. Even the appearance of failure could raise questions about his credibility and trustworthiness. As a result, he required a level of excellence in his painstaking selection of godly people to accompany the liberal gift from the Corinthian church, a foundation for success if you will, so that he and they could pass the test when judged by people or the Lord (2 Cor. 8:20–21).

The concluding verses in chapter 9 do not give the impression that financial successes or failures are the central considerations in fundraising. Paul could have outlined how much money needed to be raised or how the particular needs of the Jewish sisters and brothers would be met. For him success, although he does not use such a term, is found in a deeper understanding of God and his work in the lives of Christians. His list of what that means is extensive: the Corinthians' beneficence would ultimately result in abundant blessings; greater service; the supply, increase, enlargement, and enrichment of God's grace, resulting in greater righteousness; enrichment for greater generosity; and more praise to God. Successful fundraising on those terms may in the end have very little to do with money.

5. Need

One would assume that two biblical chapters on fundraising would include a considerable amount of information on the need, the nature of the people experiencing the need, and how the monies donated would be utilized to meet the need. Instead we have a few passing references to the importance of sharing in this service to the Lord's people in Jerusalem (2 Cor. 8:4; 9:1), an acknowledgment that the recipients will be relieved as a result of the gift (8:13), and a reminder that the relative plenty of the donors will meet the needs of the poor Jewish believers (8:14).

Since this is Paul's second letter to the Corinthians, it may be that the reason he talks so little about need is that this is not the first time they have heard about the necessity of a generous offering. In the final chapter of the first letter he references a collection and gives instructions on when it should happen, who should be involved, and how the amount should be determined, indicating that the collection will be sent to Jerusalem (1 Cor. 16:1-4). In Acts and in Romans we learn that the offering was for the poor brothers and sisters in Jerusalem (Acts 24:17; Rom. 15:26), so we might assume that the Corinthians had prior knowledge of the particular need before Paul's second letter arrived, and that his encouragements about generosity were therefore received in that context. There was no cause for him to go into all the details again.

Is Paul silent about need in 2 Corinthians 8 and 9 because he does not consider it to be crucial to an understanding of fundraising and the core tenets of philanthropy? While the generosity of the Corinthians would supply the needs of those in Jerusalem (2 Cor. 9:12), that does not seem to be what is most important. Rather, generous giving is an expression of the presence of God's grace (8:1), reflects dedication to God and to people (8:5), mirrors the downward direction in the incarnation of Jesus (8:9), and brings manifold blessings to the giver (9:6-14). Is it too extreme to say that the calling of the donor to give and the spiritual impact of generosity on those who do so may have more significance in God's economy than the need of the recipient? This may be the reason why the motivations of the fundraiser and the donor are given greater focus by the apostle than the material needs of the recipients. On the other hand, Paul is writing to effect a donation as well as describing the spiritual change that will ensue in the donors, so it is not as if those needs are completely irrelevant.

The absence of an exclusively need-centered approach would be consistent with Paul's injunctions elsewhere that Christians should recognize the unity that is inherent in the body and the shared concern that characterizes each part (1 Cor. 12:25-26), the call to share and practice hospitality with those in need (Rom. 12:13), and the importance of doing good to everyone, especially those who are brothers and sisters in Christ (Gal. 6:10). There is no obsession with the particularity of the need, the nature of the recipient, or the project under consideration. Christians connected with the triune God see their giving as rooted in their identity in him, and they live out that theological truth. There is a sense in which a call from above takes chronological precedence over responding to the needs of the other.

In the case of the Corinthians, the need that was presented to them ran even deeper than the poverty of the Jewish brothers and sisters in Jerusalem since they, as Gentiles, were participating in a much bigger drama than simply providing material help for those who were lacking basic necessities. Central to Paul's argument throughout his letters to the churches is the unity of Jew and Gentile because of their relationship with Christ (Eph. 2:11–22). The participation of the Gentile Corinthians with the Jews in Jerusalem was symbolic of that unity, and in many respects the offering was not simply about money meeting a need; rather, the offering was an exemplar of the way the church of Jesus Christ should understand itself. A generous gift would mean that the hearts of the Jewish Christians would go out to the Corinthians and they would pray for them, a posture that has less to do with friendship and relational connectedness and more to do with the primary call to unity (2 Cor. 9:14).

6. Method

What method does Paul use in his fundraising with the Corinthian church? While he does not appear to be overly interested in the details of the needs of the Jewish brothers and sisters in Jerusalem, he does want to frame the entire philanthropic emphasis in the same way he would approach any other subject worthy of biblical attention. God's grace dominates, and the Corinthians' offering is understood within the framework of Christ's descent to earth as a servant. Paul's theological argument is built around God's provision of manna in the wilderness (2 Cor. 8:15; Exod. 16:18), along with the image of the blessed man who scatters his gifts to the poor (2 Cor. 9:9; Ps. 112:9), in contrast to the image of the foolish man who sows in Proverbs (Prov. 22:8). But it would be a mistake to assume that, because of his deeply spiritual qualities and the depth of his dependence on God, Paul adopts a passive or disinterested approach to raising money and sees human effort as unimportant to his philanthropic methodology.

Paul's primary way of motivating the Corinthians is by "compare and contrast." He does that in several ways: he uses the Macedonians as an obvious point of comparison, contrasts the Corinthians' giving with other areas of their lives, shows how

Jesus's sacrificial love is different in quality from their own, and compares the actual giving of the Corinthians with their original commitment. Second Corinthians 8 does not start with an adversarial message to the church at Corinth but with an example of something different—the Macedonians, who, in spite of their struggles and poverty, gave generously even beyond Paul's expectations (2 Cor. 8:1-5). Paul commends the Corinthians for their faith, speech, knowledge, earnestness, and love but contrasts the expression of these gifts with their lack of generosity (8:7). Even the lavish love of the Lord Jesus Christ is seen as distinct from the lack of lived-out love shown by the Corinthian church (8:8-9).

His tone through both of these chapters is clear and direct. He wants the entire process to be transparent (2 Cor. 8:24), but he also wants to ensure that he is not thought to be commanding them to do something (8:8). Their giving would not be the result of excessive persuasion and manipulation, which could result in contributions being made grudgingly under duress (9:5, 7). Paul believes a valid test of their generosity is to compare them with the Macedonians (2 Cor. 8:1), and he judges that the best thing for them to do would be to finish the work they commenced (9:10-11) and come through with what they had promised (9:5).

Paul's confidence in pressing for the gift of money does not stop there, and he becomes quite personal in arguing that his boasting about them to the Macedonians is going to be hollow if they are unprepared; furthermore, regardless of their own feelings, he himself will feel ashamed (2 Cor. 9:4). While we do not have open access to Paul's emotions, it would seem that he is feeling edgy and perhaps even frustrated as he sees that the poor and persecuted Macedonians are giving generously while the Corinthians, who are blessed with strength and sufficiency, are only talking about giving but not actually making it happen.

The opening verse of chapter 9 may simply be describing reality when the apostle indicates that there is no need for him to write to them about their giving. The Corinthians had already been presented with the needs of the poor sisters and brothers in Jerusalem and had expressed their eagerness to help, so Paul indicates it would be superfluous to speak about the same subject when he has already used their previous enthusiasm to motivate the Macedonians. But is there a slightly frustrated tone present, maybe even a touch of sarcasm? If there is no need for him to write because they already know what they are doing, why include thirty-nine verses with multiple arguments for why they should come through on their commitment?

A bird's-eye view of these two chapters would suggest that Paul took every methodological detail of the fundraising enterprise seriously. In chapter 8 he outlines the philanthropic mindset of the Macedonians (2 Cor. 8:1-5), carefully examines why it is important to make good on a financial pledge (8:6-15), and gives detailed attention to the various administrative and personnel facets of the gift (8:16-24). In chapter 9 he reprises motivational comparison with the Macedonians (9:1-5), explains the results of generosity (9:6-11) and the spiritual benefits to the donor and the wider Christian community (9:12-15), all with a characteristic blend of theological and biblical expertise, along with a concern for people and a willingness to be appropriately forceful.

7. Money

You would think that the longest treatise on fundraising in the Bible would use the word *money*, but instead Paul employs terms like "service" (2 Cor. 8:4; 9:1, 13), "act of grace" (8:6), "grace of giving" (8:7), "the work" (8:11), "gift" (8:12, 20; 9:5), and "offering" (8:19), demonstrating that something as ordinary and earthbound as money can be framed and understood in more transcendent language. Once again Paul shows us how we can avoid the destructive dualism of the secular and the sacred. Such thinking would have led to a focus on the actual amount of money required by those in Jerusalem, provided by the Macedonians, or promised by the Corinthians. Yet Paul spends no time spelling out the sum needed or the monies donated. Rather, he writes that the Macedonians expressed rich generosity (8:2), gave as they were able and even beyond their ability based on their own choice (8:3), exceeded Paul's expectations in their giving to the Lord and to him (8:5), and showed a willingness to give based on their means (8:11). Similarly, the Corinthians had promised a liberal gift (8:20), a generous gift (9:5), and were invited by Paul to give an amount that they had decided in their hearts to give (9:7). Particular amounts of money have their place, but the apostle is clearly more interested in elevating other crucial aspects of fundraising so that the amount becomes more of an outcome than a goal. And Paul is on his own personal journey with money, a subject that receives considerable attention in his writings.

We know from the apostle's visit to see Aquila and Priscilla in Corinth that he, like them, was a tentmaker (Acts 18:1-3; 1 Cor. 4:12), and we assume he used whatever income he derived from that work to support himself. But, using arguments from the Hebrew Scriptures (Deut. 25:4; also quoted in the New Testament, in Luke 10:7), he is very clear with Timothy that those who provide leadership in the church should receive payment, especially those who are involved in preaching and teaching (1 Tim. 5:17-18), a point he also made to the Galatians (Gal. 6:6). When he thanks the Philippians for their ongoing support of him, support that was given multiple times and ensured that he was amply supplied, he describes it as a fragrant offering and an acceptable sacrifice but also acknowledges that they were the only church that was supporting him (Phil. 4:14-19). Furthermore, he wants them to know that he was not looking for a gift, but he wants credit to be added to their account (Phil. 4:17). In sum, the tentmaker who does not aspire for money, nor seem to need money, is receiving it. But he also advocates that others in particular roles should be given money. And whenever money is given, those who give it should have it credited to their spiritual account.

The apparent confusion in Paul's approach to fundraising is best understood by looking at the Corinthian letters in more detail, as they show that money is one of the central features of the controversy surrounding his apostolic authority. While other apostles were taking money for their ministry among the churches, Paul was supported by his tentmaking, and because of that some saw him as less than a real apostle. In the first letter he devotes almost an entire chapter to this topic and talks about the rights that pertain to apostles (1 Cor. 9:1-18). As part of that argument he indicates that, if soldiers get paid, vine keepers get to eat the grapes, and shepherds drink milk from their flock, why shouldn't those who sow spiritual seed participate in a material harvest (1 Cor. 9:7-12)? Suggesting that this is the legitimate right of the servant of the gospel, the apostle then argues that he has chosen not to use that right but is willing to preach and teach without any remuneration because he does not want to hinder the proclamation of the gospel (1 Cor. 9:12-18). Ironically, 1 Corinthians 9, one of the clearest chapters on the right of those who are serving in church ministry to be paid, actually serves to show us that Paul himself is unwilling to assume that right.

Not surprisingly, Paul's second letter to the Corinthians reminds them that he is not peddling the word of God for financial gain like the false prophets (2 Cor. 2:17), that he is continuing to serve free of charge (11:7) without being a burden on the church (11:9; 12:14, 16), and that he sees the brothers and sisters as his children who should not have to save up for their parent (12:14). The reason for his third visit to see them will not be to gain their possessions but because he loves and cares for them (12:14). If the apostle did not do the fundraising with careful attentiveness, it might create the impression that he had changed his mind and was actually raising the money for himself or using it for some other questionable reason.

The relationship between the Gentile Macedonians, the Corinthians, and the Jewish Christians in Jerusalem was of prime importance to Paul. He did not want the poor Macedonians to experience financial loss as a result of their giving, any more than he wanted the rich Corinthians to become destitute as a result of their sacrifice (2 Cor. 8:13) or the poor saints in Jerusalem to become disproportionately rich. What he wanted was equality (8:14), so that God would provide what both the Jewish and Gentile believers needed financially, and, like the children of Israel who gathered manna in the desert, everyone would have their needs met whether they gathered a little or a lot (2 Cor. 8:15; Exod. 16:13-36). In God's economy, out of his rich abundance and generosity he is not trying to make some poor and others rich; rather, God wants them to relate to one another as one body under a principle of equality where all experience divine beneficence.

FOCUSING ON THEMES

CHAPTER 3

Integration

Guiding question: Are our Christian commitments and beliefs fully integrated into every aspect of our fundraising endeavors?

Recently the two of us talked to a friend who leads a church that has grown both in depth and numbers over the last decade. Now the congregation needs to adapt their buildings in order to serve their town better, and it seems it will cost quite a lot to do it. News of their plans got out, and our friend has already been called by fundraising experts and consultants offering their services. Underlying these well-meaning overtures is the assumption that what is now needed is money and the church does not have the requisite resources to make this happen. Together we reflected on the lack of integration in that perspective. How is it that when money comes into the equation of church life we all feel we need an expert guide? What is the relationship between the emerging profession of fundraising, with its various techniques and methods, and the well-known paths that we follow in the rest of church life as we trust God, love people, and care for creation? How is it we are comfortable following those paths in most areas of our church life but seem to put raising money in a separate box?

As we saw in Paul's communication with the Corinthians, the

Christian life and all aspects of it need to be integrated around a fundamental commitment to who God is and how he functions in the world. In other words, we do not have one perspective for so-called spiritual factors, like church, prayer, or worship, and quite a different perspective for things like money, economics, and fundraising. When we talked with our friend, who was seeking to lead a church with a commitment to the authority of Scripture and the centrality of the triune God, we discovered he felt an unspoken pressure to think about the fundraising venture within a different framework. His experience is not dissimilar to our own. While the church is under the full Lordship of Christ, the raising of money for the church is often under some other canopy. We are continuing to learn in our philanthropic work not only that there is one true God but that he is over all things, not just some things.

We both continue to wrestle with the lack of integration in our own lives, but we are sure of one thing: the world of philanthropy belongs at the heart of the Christian life and cannot be safely exiled to the barren lands of secularity. If fundraising, like every other aspect of the Christian life, needs to find itself "in Christ," then our passion for a deepening knowledge of God, the community, and creation needs to overrule the temptation to focus on financial success or trust in technique. Similarly, Christian organizations and churches that have departments or designated individuals who are supposed to raise funds "for the ministry" need to drop this language and recognize that the philanthropic enterprise should be seen as integrated into the ministry, having as much need to depend on God's empowerment as any other aspect of the work.

Ironically, some deal with integration issues by being dualistic. Out of a conviction that we want to be Christian in our fundraising and have the Lordship of Christ dominate in this sphere of our functioning along with every other, two behavioral lists are created. List one is all those things that characterize fundraising that is secular, and list two outlines appropriate behavior for those who are Christian fundraisers. Our task is to follow list two and every-thing will be fine because we know what "Christian" fundraisers should do. Although so much of the Christian world adopts this pragmatic approach to living a vital spiritual life, it is inconceiv-able to be spiritually centered and yet believe that adherence to a list makes one Christian.

So what does it look like to undertake fundraising that takes its bearings from our relationship with God? Truth, in response to this question, will not lie in the simple provision of answers, or in a particular description of a method, but rather in the posing of questions. As we think about fundraising we need to ask how God fits into our understanding of ourselves, money, solicitation, donors, fundraising projects, and every other aspect of the phil-anthropic venture. It is never easy to frame the entire fundraising process, so we recognize that its purpose needs to be found within God's intentions, an approach that may slow things down and radically alter the priorities we are following. Our individual abil-ity to shape events will take a hit, and we may disappoint others who are looking for instant results and immediate funding for a particular project. But the fact that we need to ask about where God fits is not undermined by these realities.

It might seem more practical to detach the grit and grind of fundraising from godliness, which we can easily assume to be oth-erworldly in its essence. We have both experienced this in church circles where the Christian world is seen as distinct from the "real world." One of us was told by a scientist, "When I go into my lab-oratory I leave God outside the door," while a businessperson was heard to say, "I am a Christian but that is not how I function at work." In both cases God is barred from certain arenas, and ques-tions about God's passions, work, or sovereignty are ignored. A similar version of the same dynamic happens in church or para-church meetings when someone criticizes a decision by claim-ing, "you may not do it this way in the parachurch/church but in business this is how we do it," implying that the latter approach is more effective than the former. When the "real world" is separated from the church world, and the business world is distinct from the parachurch world, it begs the question of which world God is ruling over. Do we really want to function as practical atheists in a world that is the Lord's? Do we really think that God is not sovereign over money and has no perspective on it?

Language plays an important role in the struggle to embrace integration, as we have seen with terms like "ministry," "real world," and "secular." If you have spent any time in the church, you will have heard the distinction between the spiritual and the secular used on multiple occasions. At the core of this large problem is a separation of the material from the spiritual, the former imagined as linked with the body and all that is tangible and the latter referring to an otherworldly, unseen world.

It has always been tempting for Christians to detach our relationship with God from its material context despite our belief in the resurrection of the body. Jesus's demonstration of physicality in cooking and eating meals, or as he proffered the wounds of his resurrected body to Thomas's doubting, probing fingers, draws our concept of the spiritual into the very fiber of material creation and re-creation. In spite of this, so many of us are fatally drawn to idealized abstractions. Like the Colossian church, which was exposed to a Gnostic philosophy that could not countenance any link between the spiritual and the material, we need to recognize that "in Christ all the fullness of the Deity lives in bodily form" (Col. 2:9). A full understanding of the triune God will facilitate an understanding that money, a tangible and material entity, does not have to be removed from the spiritual and the transcendent but can be completely integrated into it.

A more comprehensive approach that gives God his rightful place helps us recognize that our individual encounter with a donor goes much further than a lunchtime solicitation; rather, it leads us to ask larger questions about integration. Intimate connection with the Creator involves deep engagement with creation.

Well-designed work, even for the most acute of human needs, will depend upon the sustainability of the creation on which it draws and will transform it in different ways. We habitually see our human lives in isolation from the wider creation, but if we start with the question of what God cares about, rather than what we urgently need, a better trajectory is established. Even so, the path is not straightforward. It may seem that the best way to rescue the care of creation from its currently almost exclusively secular funding would be to insist on ecology or green economics in conversation with Christians. However, while they are essential disciplines for our understanding of how life on earth is to be lived, what will draw us into knowing their significance is a truer hold on the character of God who created all things and is shaping history toward their redemption.

Through our wealth and our investments we are constantly transforming a world that is God's handiwork and not just "our" society or "our" environment. We need to recognize that all of our requests for funds have an influence on the world, a world that does not belong to us. An excessive and sole focus on financial returns runs the risk of unsustainably pressing creation to produce ever more money with no regard for the cost to creation.

In the end, a lack of integration creates fragmentation for fundraisers, and as it is communicated to donors it can become seriously unhelpful for them too. Separation between the secular and the sacred is intensified. Material matters are separated from the spiritual. Most importantly, the Lordship of Christ is eroded and his rightful place is compromised.

Like the apostle in his letter to the church at Corinth, we want to be fundraisers who bring the entire integrated perspective of the triune God to bear on every area of life, including philanthropy.

CHAPTER 4

People

Guiding question: In our work of raising funds, do we see people as being of much more value than the money they provide?

Over our years of raising funds we have received many well-intended comments along the lines of—"You should talk to her. She comes from money." "I would imagine he could fund the entire project." "I guess you will be spending a lot of time in Asia during this campaign." "There is lots of money out there." Obviously leads and advice all have their place in any sphere, and philanthropy is no different. Any of us raising funds are glad to receive suggestions, and often new connections are best made through already-established relationships. However, these four comments reflect a mindset that has caused us to pause.

When we interact with people face to face, we are exposed to a multitude of nonverbal cues—appearance, attractiveness, posture, size, shape, height, eye color, facial expressions, and the like. When they speak we hear their verbal style, language, nuancing, vocabulary, thoughts, and feelings. When we listen carefully we hear their narrative, themes, patterns, history, beliefs, and convictions. As we go deeper, the combination of these nonverbal cues with speaking and attentive listening strengthens the relationship. Mutual understanding often develops, and friendship becomes a by-product. From a theological perspective we could say we become "persons in community," living out the way God intended us to be as those created in his triune image.

Both of us have experienced this process with donors from many corners of the world. We met them either because they had an interest in the mission we were seeking to embody or because someone else had told them about that mission. In some cases, after initial engagement around money and mission, the relationship evolved and grew and we ended up becoming friends. The personal elements of the relationship transcended the professional to the degree that the financial aspect of our exchanges became quite secondary, bordering on the unimportant. At other times our initial connection with so-called donors was immediate and reciprocal, and the financial reasons for our connection became insignificant right from the beginning. These experiences led us to a simple, but we believe truly important, conclusion. Philanthropy for Christians is first about people rather than about money, the possibility of relationship rather than resources. We must stand against anything that turns persons into wallets or friends into banks.

So to say that Sally "comes from money" is to presume too much about her history and her capacity to give money at present. Sally ceases to be a person created in the image of God and instead is simply seen monochromatically through the lens of her wealth. To argue that Cecil "could fund the entire project" reflects a belief that we know what percentage of his money is available for our particular project. Cecil ceases to be a person created in the image of God but becomes someone who can meet our needs. Asserting that a trip to Asia will result in a massive amount of money coming our way is to engage in a form of subtle racism with a skewed economic grid that reads an entire geopolitical area from one perspective. Individual Asians cease to be persons created in the image of God but are reduced to being participants in a community of extravagance. Nonpersonal fundraising rises to the surface best with the oft-cited line "there is lots of money out there." Money is so detached from persons created in the image of God and made for relationship that it becomes a disembodied commodity, there for the asking and ripe for the taking.

However, there is a danger even in recognizing the importance of personal relationships. If we are persuaded that we need to give more attention to the relationships at the heart of fundraising, then we may face the risk that even this can be degraded into a necessary technique that we must master in order to become more effective. Ironically, in the pursuit of the relational, we turn it into a means to an end. We want money, we know relationships are important, so let's be relational so we can get the money. We see such corruptions taking hold even on the holy ground of sharing the gospel as we encounter such perverse phrases as "friendship evangelism," which force grace to serve a programmatic end. But the risk of operationalizing authentic relationships will be avoided if the foundational relationship that the fundraiser attends to is not with potential donors but with God himself. He is the one who is calling us to the work that needs funding, and it is the truth of our relationship with him that will spill over into the human relationships between donors and fundraisers as they meet and encounter each other's concerns. We value people, and the relationships that ensue, not because of people's capacity to give but because they are created in God's image, and our community with them is therefore inevitable.

This posture is not unique to the world of philanthropy but is exactly how all our encounters with others should be ordered. Just as evangelism can be undertaken in ways that betray the very nature of a loving gospel, by the use of manipulation, bribery, or propaganda, so fundraising can suffer from a similar set of blemishes, even when undertaken for good causes. Nothing but a greater attention to the God who is the unique source of true transformation for people and creation will spare us from the temptation of only affording people dignity, or giving them respect, if they are blessed with wealth or influence. In much of the world relationships have degenerated into trading, and friendships are sustained to the extent that they serve people's interests, but the Christian community, which has been borne and sustained by grace, is the last place where that should happen.

Such a perspective is particularly challenging when we are trying to establish priorities in our fundraising. Where should we wisely give our time? If we fundraise in ways that are coherent with our understanding of the character of God and the value of people, does it still make sense to aim to spend more time with those who have high financial capacity? Jesus commended the widow for giving her mite (Luke 21:1-4) and, as the Old Testament prophets had done, he reserved some of his most forceful warnings for the rich (Luke 6:25), and even their apparent generosity (Mark 12:41-44). Christian organizations above a certain size frequently have fundraising departments, and they often structure these departments around a paradigm that links low-level donors with particular staff and high-capacity givers with the CEO, suggesting that there may be relational consequences for giving more or less.

Simple answers are not easily found for this conundrum. While we continue to enjoy friendships and fundraising discussions with people who we know have little capacity to give financially, we are also aware that those who are intending to make a major financial contribution need time to get to know us and understand our organizational mission. Major new income always makes an impact on any organization, and careful conversations are needed over time so donors can ensure that their contribution is going to make the difference they desire. On the other hand, we have both spent a lot of time with new friends who have discovered our different projects but who are never going to make major gifts. Over many years we have seen that these relationships have consequences for the kingdom that go far beyond financial capacity, and we want to prize them for those reasons. Attentiveness to these wider stories, as we will recount later, has made our own fundraising into a far more fruitful and creative ministry than merely raising money.

To the extent that we make money our relational metric, we diminish our actual relationships with God, people, and creation—and it is our human privilege to enjoy and deepen them all. A simple search for money is more akin to mere consumerism, and it is not surprising that wealthy people who have been on the receiving end of it can feel that they are only appreciated for their money. If we who raise funds cannot separate people from their money and friends from funds, we actually begin to abuse people by making them feel that their wallet is the only thing that matters in the relationship. Often these donors already feel quite estranged and alone because it is hard to develop genuine relationships in which they are seen for who they are and not for what they have. This is particularly true of people with significant wealth who are approached on a daily basis and consequently have to develop strategies of protecting themselves from others. While staff, websites, and elaborate application forms may protect wealthy donors at a very practical level, the mere existence of these more institutionally oriented mechanisms further exacerbates relational distance and intensifies loneliness. We have both known wealthy people who have told us that they actually avoid churches, Christian communities, and social settings because they are perceived as an embodied wallet.

In many respects, a relational approach to fundraising is an invitation to the donor not just to give money, but to participate in the community they are supporting. While we recognize the risk of donors seeking to buy influence, either through giving their gift or threatening to withhold it, those who give to our work need to be seen as part of us, as connected with the mission and the ministry, not as those outside who provide money from a distance. We have talked with those who do not welcome this engagement, but they are in the minority. Might it be that the loneliness and isolation of the wealthy could be eased by the disinterested welcome and hospitality of a receiving community who are deeply aware that their provision comes finally from God rather than from their donors? Maybe we need to stop talking about the donors who are going to support our mission, our need, our campaign as a group somehow apart, and see them as part of "us," an integral aspect of the "we" that is seeking to pursue our kingdom mission as the body of Christ.

In spite of this emphasis, we also need to recognize that there will be times when the donor is not in close relationship to the organization and there is an absence of mutuality and intimacy. Because of geographical distance, health, mobility, or other legitimate factors, a donor might be unable to be part of the community that is receiving the gift. In those cases it would be inappropriate to suggest that funders who are removed are less worthy givers or are missing the central feature of a personal engagement with giving. And it also should be noted that the relational boundaries are set by the invitation of the donors; fundraisers who ignore those constraints and the ethical guidelines of philanthropy, and so become overly enmeshed in their personal connection with donors, or enchanted by the privileged environment of the wealthy, are unlikely to be able to work virtuously.

Like the apostle in his letter to the church at Corinth, we want to be fundraisers who see donors not as instrumental in helping us reach our goal, but as those who are created in the image of God and are a central aspect of our mission.

CHAPTER 5

Work

Guiding question: Do we position our fundraising work in the bigger story of God's work in the world?

Fundraising is hard work. Not hard work in the sense of long hours, travel, multiple meetings, or a full schedule, all of which are true. It is hard work in a different way. We have both faced times when we have had no idea how our organizations could find essential funds, not just for new work that we felt was important, but even to maintain what we were doing. Anxiety under these constant pressures, a sense of uncertainty and insecurity, and a persistent awareness of institutional need made these seasons hard. What if there was not enough money for a given project, for payroll, for annual requirements? We have both worked in organizations where relationships were highly valued, and many of those who could lose their jobs if we failed financially had become our friends. If we carry the burden of leadership in fundraising we will face countless questions about people, money, and need, but if we do our leadership well it can also cause us to reflect fruitfully on the nature of the work itself.

In most organizations, metrics are established around fundraising. Frequently budgets are constructed, and one line reads

"Donations." On receipt of that particular figure, fundraisers set out to find the resources to meet the budget. Based on a slightly different approach, some institutions establish a "number of visits" metric, where fundraisers are expected to have face-to-face visits with twelve to fifteen people in a month. Technologically based fundraising may specify a "number of visits to the website" approach, and the fundraisers need to ensure they are maximizing the likelihood of that transpiring. Crowdsourcing, or the less personal solicitation of funds usually through an online community, is often assessed by how close the amount raised comes to the specified target.

Answering the question "What is your work?" will vary depending on the approach that is taken to metrics: "My work is to raise x dollars"; "My work is to make fourteen visits this month"; "My work is to cultivate website hits." Our question is, does raising dollars, making visits, and cultivating hits constitute the sum total of our work, or is there something else going on? If, as we have argued earlier, fundraising should grapple with the same questions and issues that are characteristic of the rest of the Christian life, then a core question needs to be asked: As we seek to please God in our work, how much are our own efforts needed and how much comes down to God's grace and work? When Christians raise questions such as these about healing or prayer, the conclusions are obvious. It seems to be entirely of God and has little to do with our agency and initiative. Is fundraising any different?

Glancing back at history, we have the examples of George Muller and Hudson Taylor, who saw fundraising as so completely God's work that they felt it better not to make their needs known and so never directly solicited funds. By contrast, the apostle Paul and William Wilberforce were among those who approached the solicitation of money systematically and with candid persistence. In all cases their varying convictions were not based on choices about method but on conclusions about God's calling and direction. The question therefore is surely not whether there is one place we find ourselves on a spectrum that runs from an exclusive reliance on our hard work at one end to passively waiting for the acts of God at the other. Our own experience has taught us that, while diligence and creativity are necessary in our work, we ultimately need to affirm that the work is of God and that whatever fruit may come is ultimately linked with his grace and mercy. In many respects it is the dance of the both-and rather than the opposition of the either-or.

Just as the person who thinks it wrong to put any effort beyond personal prayer into raising funds ought reasonably to avoid consulting a doctor if they get sick, so anyone who accepts that farmers need to sow seed in their fields if they are to hope for a harvest should have no trouble with the idea of asking for money. As persons who believe both that God is at work in his world and that he delights to work with and through us, we have found that fundraising has brought these issues to the surface in helpful ways, and they have informed our overall Christian life. We have both been delightfully baffled when major financial provision arrives out of left field from people we had never expected to help, while well-planned requests have failed. We have frequently had donor meetings where our preparation was impeccable, our written material of high quality, and our financial request clear and direct, but we have left with no gift. In contrast, we have often rejoiced over a substantial gift that came without any energy expended on our side, and we were left with the feeling that all we could do was express gratitude to God.

We have both been part of organized teams submitting major grant proposals to institutions where all the criteria seemed to be met; on some occasions the grant was given, and on other occasions, because of circumstances that were out of anyone's control, the application failed. We have known inexplicable moments of both grace and confusion. It is easy to misjudge the likely response of those we hope will support the work we care passionately about, even when we have worked hard to inform and interest

Like those who find themselves in a battle, we need to recognize that human agency and effort contribute to what is happening. Feeding, grooming, resting, and arming the horse are all integral to waging war. If we sit in the stable, ignore the horse, and do not bear arms, the chances of defeating the enemy are minimal. On the other hand, even if we prepare the horse well and win the battle, we cannot trace the victory back to our efforts.

For us, the best way to keep watch over ourselves in this realm is to examine the spirit in which we do our work in fundraising. If we are sloppy and lazy, unmotivated and disinterested, it is unlikely that much will happen. However, if we are frantic, anxious, and fretting, believing that our intensity is going to bring about results, we have missed the heart of the Christian message. When our work takes on a tone of being wound up and highly strung, we become bundles of hyperactivity, talking to donors, making requests, monitoring results, and believing deep down that outcomes are tied to the depth of our passion and the busyness of our schedule. Like the church worker who experiences compassion fatigue because of her desire to meet the needs of everyone, or the businessperson who is in a compulsive rush to every meeting, the fundraiser can be tempted to live as if spending an inordinate amount of time getting the horse ready is going to result in a battle that will inevitably be won.

Contemplative work in a garden allows us to till the soil, provide some water, get rid of the weeds, and provide fertilizer, all the while realizing that our work as a gardener is not to make the plant grow. That is the responsibility of the God of the universe, who has the sole responsibility of creating, sustaining, and giving the increase, a reality that allows us to do our part without shrinking back on the one side, or being obsessively overwrought on the other. In essence, our work as fundraisers is not only to raise a certain amount of money, make a specified number of visits, or cultivate a particular number of hits on the website, important as those may be. Our work is to be in tandem with the triune God, who not only knows the financial needs of our organizations and the monetary capacity of all donors but is also aware of the full range of the needs of both those who give and those who receive. It takes very little reflection for us to realize that they go well beyond the material and financial in both cases.

Like the apostle in his letter to the church at Corinth, we want to be fundraisers who are working in step with the living God who is building his kingdom, sometimes using our initiative and diligence to make that happen, and at other times not using them at all.

CHAPTER 6

Success

Guiding question: In the kingdom work of fundraising, is the financial outcome the only measure of success and failure?

Fundraisers usually experience a surge of inner excitement in response to the "Yes, I will give," a quiet hopefulness to the "Maybe later," and reflective or sometimes acute disappointment to the "No, I will not be giving to this project." However understandable these reactions may be, they are not the end of the story for most of us. As we hang up from the donor phone call, walk away from the lunch meeting, or drive back to the office, we often ask a more fundamental question—was I successful?

Success is a beguiling concept in contemporary culture. We all seem to want it, aspire to it, and revel in it, and we live in fear of the alternative—failure. Our own experience as fundraisers mirrors this perspective all too well. However, this is not unlike the rest of our Christian life, as we want to be seen as successful whether it be as leaders, administrators, counselors, pastors, teachers, or, in Peter's case, conservationists! Lurking deep in our souls is this childlike ambition to be forever linked with the word *successful* and never to be thought of as failures.

Simplistic and binary as the distinction between success and failure may be, it has generated important issues for us as we have sought to raise money. As soon as judgment is pronounced on a given activity, and terms like "success" and "failure" are used, we are forced to ask what metrics are being used, are these appropriate metrics, and who is using them? If a metric like the amount of dollars is the sole basis for assessing the success of the philanthropic enterprise, basic arithmetic skills combined with a specified number will allow us to determine if we have failed or not. But surely there is more to it than that, especially for those of us who want to do our fundraising in a way that honors Christ.

Given that there are so many components to fundraising, we need to ensure that all of them, and not just the financial outcome, are assessed carefully. Is the organization functioning well missionally, relationally, and spiritually? Is the case well thought through and carefully argued? Is there a genuine experience of real dependence on God in the preparatory phases for the case and the request for money? Is the connection with the donor respectful, personal, and filled with integrity? Is the right amount of information provided so that an appropriate decision can be made? These are all critical success factors that can get lost in a preoccupation with "Did we get the money?" even if all of these elements may be completed superbly and no money comes in.

We recognize in our own psyches a temptation to allow the metrics of others to influence our sense of well-being. Both of us have been seen as successful fundraisers by some, but others have seen us as failures. We assume, even in writing this book, that our supporters will be glad we are putting our philanthropic experience into print, while our detractors will question our credibility given that we never raised enough money. Naturally such a paradigm has made us anxious at times, even fearful that if we do not raise enough money for what our colleagues need and hope for, not only will they consider us to be failures, but we will draw the same conclusion ourselves. Again, this is not discontinuous with our entire Christian life. How do we do any work as Christians without being lured into the temptation to control outcomes, yearn for accolades, and hope for certainty?

When financial metrics are the prime measure of success, everyone involved, including the donors, will be confirmed in their conviction that money is the answer to the organization's needs. Unhelpfully for the egos of all concerned, the supposed ability or techniques of the fundraiser or the generosity of the donor become the key to true security. Money becomes the solution, the way forward. Relationships then slip deeply into the shadows of unreality where we trust in our own success stories rather than finding our place within the wider story of God's purposes and his provision. Because the real world is God's world, lovingly created so that all can live by relationships that are rooted in his character and care, we will be on a road to grief if we press creation out of its true relational shape and turn money into the answer for all organizational maladies.

Entitlement is the fertile soil in which these kinds of attitudinal errors develop. When we assume that we need something and it is owed to us, expectations are created, and we begin to believe the advertising slogan—"You deserve it." Slipping into the mindset, either as individuals or organizations, that we deserve money allows us to ignore fundamental realities in the Christian life. If all of life and everything in it can be traced to the Creator and there is a recognition that we do not deserve anything, we start to glimpse the truth that everything is gift. We are recipients of God's grace and goodness, both of which are rooted in his character, and even when we fall short and are not deserving of his gifts, his mercy overwhelms us. All of the Christian life, including fundraising, needs to find its bearings by having gift, grace, and gratitude at the center.

Imagine a philanthropic world where those needing money had a posture toward our God of gift, grace, and gratitude; where those asking for money recognized that they are operating in a context in which God's grace and goodness overflow and they can trust him, not donors, to meet all their needs; where those giving money saw their resources as flowing not from their own work, investments, or financial savvy but from God, their sustainer and provider, who has given them his money to steward for the good of his kingdom. A paradigm shift of this nature would turn the fundraising transaction into something transcendent and would make the use of terms like "success" and "failure" irrelevant at best, and irreverent at worst.

As we walk away from donor meetings we can easily make premature, earthbound judgments of success and failure. But what would happen if in confident prayer we came to realize that we are not in command of the outcome? "Nos" and "maybes" would not be cause for consternation but could provoke a settled sense that God is in control; that he understands what is needed for the organization, fundraiser, and donor; and that he will do his work in his time. Anxiety would be replaced by prayer and pessimism by hope.

Feedback from those around us, often based on other metrics, would not cause us discouragement. We would recognize that the final judgment, God's sole prerogative, is not just an assessment of what we did wrong on this planet but the final conclusion of what we did right. A particular donor meeting may not show immediate results that can be applauded either by us or by onlookers, but there may be a day when this meeting bears fruit that we will not know about. But God will.

What we need to do is learn to separate goals and desires when it comes to our philanthropic work. Goals are pursuits that we, under the providence of God, can completely control and thus can be held accountable for their accomplishment. So, as a parent, I might make it my goal to have my children turn out well, but if I do, I have failed to realize that I cannot completely control this outcome. There are too many factors that influence the behavior of a child, and, sadly, parenting is only one of them. In contrast, what if parents were to say, I want to be the best parent I can be?

That is worthy of pursuit because I know it is something I can control and has nothing to do with how the children turn out.

While this may make conceptual sense, the reality is that all parents want their children to turn out well. That aspiration is not a goal but a desire. A desire is a pursuit that is influenced by the agency of others, so we cannot be held totally responsible. And unlike a goal, where work is expended to achieve a particular result, a desire invites prayer. Any of us who have parented know the incredible tension between these two perspectives. On the one hand, I am working hard to achieve the goal of being the best parent I can be, but on the other I am praying feverishly that God will grant me my desire to see my children turn out well. I know that, no matter how well I pursue my goal of being a good parent, I cannot guarantee the fruit of my desire: well-behaved children. But it is quite straightforward actually. Work toward your goals. Pray into your desires.

Similarly, as fundraisers we might pray, desire, and wish for a particular gift from a specific donor at just the right time, and consider the accomplishment of that as a success, but we cannot control that outcome. Hence the raising of funds is more about desires than about goals. That is the great angst for every raiser of funds. No matter how good you are as a fundraiser, you cannot guarantee that a gift is forthcoming.

However, if we do not turn our desires into goals, then we can focus on the right thing. Recognizing who God is in this process, and embracing gift, grace, and gratitude, allows us to enter into the world of fundraising with a posture that it is his work and he is the main actor, while we play our minor part. No doubt we will bring our prayer to God asking him to grant our desire for a gift, but we will also bring our prayer to him asking him to work in what we ask for, how we ask for it, and how we will respond to the yes, no, or maybe response. These are fundraising goals that we can work toward as they are bathed in prayer.

In the final analysis, maybe prayer is the best way forward. In prayer we come to realize who God is, how he works, and what he wants. In prayer we see who we are, how we work, and what we want. In prayer we realize how those two realities come into sharp distinction, how our knowledge of ourselves and our knowledge of God are worlds apart, how our ways of fundraising are not his ways and his ways are not our ways. One of the outcomes of a prayerful posture before God is the recognition that our understandable absorption with financial success can be replaced by reveling in faithfulness, and the fear of failure needs to be replaced by resting in grace. Not only would this revolutionize Christian fundraising, but it would reorient all of our activities in the work of the kingdom.

Like the apostle in his letter to the church at Corinth, we want to be fundraisers who move away from the oppression of evaluative schemes based solely on financial success and failure, into a sphere where gift, grace, and gratitude invite us into faithful service.

CHAPTER 7

Need

Guiding question: If we emphasize the needs we are seeking to meet, do we risk negating God's calling and priorities for both asker and giver?

"Now that we are on the field," the missionary letter said, "we need a new jeep, and we wondered if you would make a donation to ensure that this happens." "We need more space for our drop-in center," the fundraiser explained, and then went on to spell out why donors were obliged to meet that need. As the pastor outlined the importance of adding a new staff member so the needs of the community could be met, the church was asked to come the following week with tithes and offerings, over and above their regular contribution, so this goal could be realized.

All of these examples are connected by the idea of "need," a phenomenon that pervades Western culture. "Need" is the touchstone for so much of our lives. We often hear from those who have left marriages or unsatisfying work, "She was not meeting my needs," or "They did not meet my needs." The revolving door that seems to be a feature of many city churches is often explained by those coming in or out as "that church was not meeting our needs." Why is this framing of life so captivating to us? Why are others responsible for the meeting of my needs? Why has fund-

Need

raising adopted the same attitude, so that those with needs approach those with means in such a way that it becomes the duty of the latter to assuage the demands of the former?

When American psychologist Abraham Maslow birthed his "hierarchy of needs" paradigm in the 1940s and '50s, he may not have realized that its influence would extend well beyond the social science community. His premise was that we as autonomous individuals all have needs that are understood best in a hierarchy. Our most basic needs—survival, safety, and belongingness—should be met first; only after these basic needs are met could the higher needs of respect and self-actualization be achieved. In other words, to be the best that one can be, to be oneself, to reach one's full potential, all of which are summarized by the term "self-actualization," our needs at the lower levels should be met first.

One of the main critiques of this framework is that Maslow's perspective is individualized and does not take into account the collective or the community. When my personal needs become ultimate, and when I am striving to be the best that I can be, others can become secondary. The common good is not elevated; rather, my own self-actualization is overvalued, and my potential for being "who I am" is considered priority number one. The logic of Maslow's argument creates a group of individuals, quite absorbed with their own individual needs, who carry a sense of entitlement and who view others as those whose primary purpose is to meet those needs. Parents of infants or young children, who have the responsibility to feed, change, cuddle, encourage, and do all manner of things to ensure that all the needs of their child are met, understand the sense of weariness and disquiet that results over time when your entire life is consumed by meeting needs. It is noteworthy that infants are incapable of factoring in the common good but are only focused, in their developing brains, on what is best for them.

Exacerbating this social challenge in contemporary culture is the shift of the word *need* from a verb to a noun. When we say,

"I need water, food, and shelter," *need* functions as a verb. Technically the verb *need* is not an action verb—I ran for the food—but is a stative verb that expresses a state or condition, a description of the way things are. We really do need water, food, and some sort of shelter to survive. Maslow's first level of needs makes sense.

However, what about these sentences? "I have a need for achievement." "I have a need for sex." "I have a need for things." "I have a need for money." *Need* is now a noun, a person/place/thing, and it is built on a deficiency platform. I may be lacking achievement, sex, things, or money, but by framing them as needs there is an implicit assumption that these needs must be met. Since I, the private autonomous individual, am short on achievement, sex, things, and money, it becomes the role of the other or the community to meet those needs. And if I have adopted this cultural norm, I will have an inner conviction that I am entitled to have those needs met and that you, or someone else, has an obligation to meet them. Here we have the ingredients for a deadly brew, with needs as the flavor to which we add a large cup of entitlement and a full liter of obligation. But is there another way?

> Very early in the morning, while it was still dark, Jesus got up, left the house and went off to a solitary place, where he prayed. Simon and his companions went to look for him, and when they found him, they exclaimed: "Everyone is looking for you!" Jesus replied, "Let us go somewhere else—to the nearby villages—so I can preach there also. That is why I have come." So he traveled throughout Galilee, preaching in their synagogues and driving out demons. (Mark 1:35-39)

Experiencing what many leaders go through—namely, the presentation of needs in the phrase "Everyone is looking for you"—Jesus utters startling words. "Let us go somewhere else." What about the needs that are right in front of you? What about the fact that everyone is looking for you? Are you not here to meet our needs, Jesus? Is that not what your ministry is about? Apparently not. Jesus got up early, before the sun arose, and found a quiet place so he could commune with the Father. Not obsessed with the horizontal presentation of needs, he was more in tune with the vertical call from his Father. His prayerful attentiveness was not a "look out" perspective so he could absorb and meet all the needs of people. Rather, it was a "look up" viewpoint so he knew what the Father was calling him to do. Obedience to the Father always directed how he met the needs of people. It is arresting for all of us to realize that Jesus passed by many people who had needs that he did not address. Whatever it may mean to follow Jesus, it certainly cannot mean that everyone is going to have their needs met by my ministry.

Through the aggressive "development" of globalization, media saturation, and technological advances, philanthropic needs are becoming more and more obvious. Within this globally connected Christian community, individuals and communities are far more easily able to make all their needs known, and donors are feeling the dual pressure of entitlement from the fundraisers and obligation in themselves. In the process, both those who request the money and those who provide it are realizing that meeting all these needs is an impossible journey and that even Jesus, with all the resources of heaven, was not the ultimate meeter of needs.

An alternative is needed where *calling* takes priority over *need*, where careful attentiveness to the Father is not an added extra to fundraising interactions, but is the core of the conversation. Then prayer becomes a shared process in which the fundraiser is seeking God's face on the viability of the project and the donor is communicating with the same God, ascertaining the best way to steward funds. We could understand God's will, not as an individual process whereby God tells me what I need and then I tell you what you should do with your money, but as a shared belief that God is the beginning and end of all my projects and the beginning and end of all philanthropic pursuits. Then we can focus on shared participation in what God is doing rather than the deification of our plans or our provision. When these things happen, needs are not the most important factor in the fundraising world; instead, they are understood in a larger context where the call of God helps us interpret and understand the nature of the needs and whose calling it may be to meet them.

Like the apostle in his letter to the church at Corinth, we want to be fundraisers who are attentive to God's call in the life of the organization that is seeking funds as well as in the lives of the people who are providing those funds.

CHAPTER 8

Method

Guiding question: Does an overemphasis on techniques in fundraising blind us to the reality that both askers and givers need to pay careful attention to the call of God in the process?

A televangelist tells his audience that they will receive prayer if they make a financial donation, and a parachurch organization uses a celebrity to promote their particular product. A donor is offered a seat at the Board table, and organizations use graphics and language that oversell a specific cause. All these well-known practices raise the important question of the relationship between means and ends. Should we spend as much time and energy in thinking through *how* we raise money as we do on how much money we raise?

In philosophy this topic is known as the "purification of means," which considers not just which means are appropriate to achieve a given end, but how they can be employed in a way that is coherent with the end itself. So, in our first example of the corruption of means, prayer, which is necessarily conducted between the Creator and the created, becomes directly linked with giving money, and as a result prayer is inevitably presented as something one can buy. Similarly, if a celebrity—well known for reasons unrelated to the cause, such as appearance, status, power, or success—raises money for an organization that is committed to the poor and marginalized, is there a tension between the means and the ends? If, as we have argued, fundraising needs to be about who God is and implies a particular understanding of those central themes discussed above, we should expect the way we raise money to be influenced by this same understanding.

Christians have to take into account methodological and technical considerations as they fundraise, but these are secondary to the relationship with the triune God that fundraiser and giver share. Such an approach requires us to learn the ways of God within the limitations of our partial vision until the kingdom finally comes. The vulnerability and clear dependence on God and other people that both fundraising and good giving imply furnish us with a well-crafted set of spurs to urge us into this endeavor. We are persuaded that all work requires preparation in God's presence before methodological considerations come into play. In practical terms this means conscious prayer, reflection, and study along with decision-making in community—these become our shared commitments as we find God's ways forward. For us it is essential that the preparation of the fundraiser and the donor for this demanding task begins God-ward, continues in community, and only then looks out to the giver or the receiver.

Such an approach is not only theoretically wise, and well grounded theologically, but also makes practical sense. It is often said that people give to people, and the extent to which we ourselves embody the work we care about will become very apparent. However, it is also true that people give to vision, and the kinds of visions that compel generosity are formed in the knowledge of the character of God, and out of deep engagement with creation and with human community. Once again a paradox appears—funding might seem a merely mechanical requirement for a set of tasks that impose themselves, but in reality it is the other way around. As we learn more of who God is and what he cares about, we find ourselves in a deepening relationship where we begin to glimpse how we might find the finances and other resources that are needed to bring vision into material realities. Both of us have had the experience of a person coming to mind as someone who might be interested in supporting a project, and the idea arrived almost as poets sometimes describe their poems—something ready formed and almost with a life of its own. The resultant gift had little to do with our strategy or method but seemed to be a divine appointment orchestrated by God himself, with the fundraiser and the donor simply showing up. In this, as in many other areas of our work, we have found the ministry of the Holy Spirit in giving us particular gifts of insight, and even, with a very small *p*, prophecy, critically important.

Attentiveness to God and a corresponding trust in his purposes and timing will release those giving or seeking money from one of our worst enemies—anxiety. Philanthropists' anxiety about the appropriate use of their money and fundraisers' anxiety about the funding of their work put unreasonable pressure on money to be the answer to a multiplicity of needs. If fundraisers present themselves as the needy victims, and the donor as the messiah, it will do violence to the true identity of both. If donors are tempted to believe that they alone hold the key to meeting the needs of the organization they want to help, it will corrupt the relationship at the outset. Anxiety leads us to ignore the relational truths and context of the discussions that need to find their place under the canopy of God's grace, and so we can be tempted to push ourselves to arrive at a final result in the fastest possible time.

We have heard from many donors that good fundraisers are able to slow down in order to listen, and so we suspect there should be a slow fundraising movement to match the virtues of the slow food movement. Eating was never intended to be merely a way of fueling up the body, and agriculture cannot be reduced to a simple process where soil and climate turn plants and animals into food. In the same way, fundraising is an opportunity for many of the things that good food and organic agriculture are about—respect for local conditions and relationships, fellowship, the husbandry of time, and a way for those who care about the world in similar ways to exchange far more than money, and find ways of discovering encouragement and wisdom in their journey together under God.

Does all this talk about attentiveness to God and the ways he works have any practical value? As we prepared to write this book, we talked to people with private funds, people who run foundations, and people who are responsible for corporate philanthropy, and they all agreed on one thing. The fundraisers they valued most highly were those who demonstrated a capacity to listen and to understand what the donors wanted their giving to achieve. Sadly, however, all agreed that it was far more normal for them to meet fundraisers who were in "sales mode," eager to impress with the virtues of the work of their organizations, and frequently quite poor listeners with little interest in learning about the concerns of the donor. Strategy seemed to replace relationship, and method was more about doing than about being present.

As we reflect upon method, we would argue that listening, not telling, is the primary posture of the fundraiser, not simply in company with people but with God himself. He is the one who is calling us to the work that needs funding, and it is the truth of our relationship with him that will spill over into the human relationships between donors and fundraisers as they encounter each other's concerns. The foundation of all listening skills will be attentiveness to God, which will naturally characterize all our other relationships. This, of course, is exactly how encounters and discussions between believers and others about faith should be ordered, so it should be familiar ground for Christians. And yet, just as evangelism can be carried out in ways that betray the very nature of a loving gospel, by the use of manipulation, bribery, propaganda, or human control, so fundraising can suffer from a similar set of blemishes, even when undertaken for good causes.

Only greater attention to God, who alone is the source of true transformation for people and creation, will spare us from the temptations of false power in both evangelism and fundraising.

Like the apostle in his letter to the church at Corinth, we want to be fundraisers who recognize that our primary responsibility is not the utilization of techniques and methods but an attentiveness to the work of God in our lives as well as in the lives of donors.

CHAPTER 9

Money

Guiding question: Do we understand money simply as a transaction in the fundraising process or as something transformative for all concerned?

It is not insignificant that our last theme is money. Given the usual approach to fundraising, one would think that money should be the first and primary focus, but we believe it needs to follow thoughtful wrestling with all we have considered about integration, people, work, success, need, and method. In a sense money is a by-product of other, more important dynamics.

Any significant social movement or effort for transformation needs someone to provide the initial trusting investment and to pay the bills. Without the oxygen of financial backing, it is extremely hard to sustain any kind of organization. While Jesus's own supporters seem to have given less in money and more in kind—rooms, food, the donkey in Jerusalem—he clearly expected giving and receiving to be a normal part of how his own work would be accomplished. In this way, Jesus's expectations were set within a particular time and culture—drawing on the contemporary ideas of meals, landscape, family, farming, and language in order to express the timeless truths of the kingdom of God.

74

But we miss the point if we think that the observable and obvious manifestation of giving and receiving is simply about the material exchange of money or goods. Jesus consistently relativized these cultural realities by referencing his kingdom. All Christians find that the Bible holds up the earthiness of our lives to a more searching and universal examination that seeks God's character above all. The way we live with our money or lack of it is no different.

An integrated perspective does not see money as something neutral that is given from one person to another and has nothing to do with spirituality or an understanding of our relationship with God. Once we ask for money or give money, we are moving into the realm of what is important, what matters, what counts, what we value. Within that context Jesus's words make considerable sense:

> No one can serve two masters. Either you will hate the one and love the other, or you will be devoted to the one and despise the other. You cannot serve both God and money. (Matt. 6:24)

Money can be worshiped, served, and handled in such a way that it commands our affection and commitment and becomes our focus.

When individuals and organizations, and their philanthropic community, make financial success the key and primary outcome of fundraising, they have slipped into a mindset that is potentially dangerous. We can become enveloped in a perspective where more money is best and less money is problematic, and we pay little if any attention to other variables. Organizations can begin to assume that their mission, and their execution of the mission, is inherently good and out of that self-satisfied perspective claim that money "is all we need." Pressure is then placed on fundraisers to bring in more money, and donors are expected to provide more, so the self-perception is confirmed—money is all we need. While often residing in an unconscious attitude, such an approach creates dependence on funds rather than on God, with the result that money becomes worshiped because it is our master. Sadly, such a scenario can occur whether the organization is flush with funds and has money left over every fiscal year, or whether they are always feeling the financial pinch and are hoping for more.

Financial gains that meet our own criteria for success are only too possible, and in most societies those are the ones that attract the most acclaim. The dominant measure of success in rich and poor worlds is financial, and so other forms of accounting are at a severe discount. Many churches and parachurch organizations will actually use money raised as one of the metrics of success and in so doing forget that our own spiritual transformation, the transformation of our personal relationships, and the transformation of the world are all crucial when it comes to the giving and receiving of money. Money actually provides us with a context, or an occasion, to have our values, commitments, and priorities revealed and the nature of our spiritual transformation exposed.

If those who raise funds seek to live an integrated Christian life, to value people in a way that is separate from money, to see their work as being done in tandem with the triune God, to measure success with metrics suffused in grace, to frame their service in terms of call rather than need, and to have attentiveness to the work of God rather than mere technique, they have laid a solid foundation for how to deal with money. They will not link money with status and significance—for themselves, their organizations, or their potential funders—nor will they make financial claims for themselves or others that are independent of God's evaluation. Recognizing that Scripture provides plenty of encouragement not to measure people by their money, we need to keep God in focus, people primary, and creation foundational, all of which provides a seedbed to grow our understanding of what it means to be human apart from the presence or the absence of money.

Such a perspective will drive us into larger questions about the use of money in God's wider world, and we will not just be consumed about fundraising for our own private projects and organizations. While local and personal concerns have their value, the challenge becomes how to bring financial resources to bear on the massive global problems that now confront us all. Certainly transformation, biblically understood, begins with our inmost being, but our biblical imaginations will be weakened if our vision of transformation ends there. As we keep our own hearts turned toward our Creator, we recover our sense of community, both with those around us and with far wider concerns. That in turn prevents our relationship to money from being lived out privately and allows it to come under the loving gaze of God. In that light, we will have a far more real view of the nature of our material lives and financial choices, recognizing that this world does not belong to us.

Prompted by God's Spirit, we can then be free to ask more about the ethical relationship between wealth creation and the provision of philanthropic funds. If God cares about all things and not just some people or some things, is it appropriate, as some historic philanthropists have famously done, to turn dark decades of enrichment at the expense of the poor and the planet into benevolent years of generosity? How do we respond to those who may observe ethical criteria in their private lives, but when it comes to business or personal investing believe that "good stewardship" requires them to make financial return the only responsible measure, with no regard for the creational cost? If our wealth and our investments are constantly transforming a world that is God's handiwork and not just "our" society or "our" environment, to what degree are we using our money to drive people into poverty and various species to extinction? Nor are nonprofits exempt from the same searching questions—they too have investment policies and live out their work in very material ways. Their way of working and stewarding their resources will always have an impact for better or worse on the wider creation. However, we have often found that they may be unaccustomed to considering the broader implications of their choices when it comes to their own organizational life and culture. They are also frequently unaware that their activities and identities are being noted more directly than their words or publications. This is particularly true in a world that is very connected by social media. So the question of what kind of witness we are to the God we serve is given insufficient attention. The key is to follow the biblical advice, "avoid all appearance of evil" (1 Thess. 5:22).

Like the apostle in his letter to the church at Corinth, we want to be fundraisers who recognize that money is not simply transactional, something to get in order to fund our project, but one aspect of our Christian lives that will, on a large or small scale, be transformative for people, our communities, and the planet.

OFFERING OUR STORIES

CHAPTER 10

Peter's Story

Contradictory views within my family formed my own attitudes to money, giving, and then fundraising, as I suppose they have done for many others. The class system still played a major role in British childhoods of the 1950s and '60s, and my family had effectively formed around two classes. My father came from London and a privileged background but one that, like Rod's, had inherited paradoxical and conflicted views about how wealth was earned, spent, or given. His own father had become a Christian I know not how, but within essentially Brethren spirituality; the fault-lines within that particular section of the church can be traced back to the conflicts and varied currents that made themselves felt in the earliest days of the Reformation.[1]

This particular strand of the British church was in some senses at the cutting edge of determined discipleship in the 1930s, when much of the Anglican Church was languishing under the influence of liberal theology and Freemasonry. While my father moved more into the theological mainstream in adult life, finally becoming an evangelical Anglican after a short spell with the Methodists—a typical middle-class trajectory—the different tracks remained in parallel rather than merging. And another influence played a major part in forming his responses to all things financial. The austerities and losses of those who lived through World War II, when he was a pilot on bomber squadrons, gave him a wry perspective on the thoughtless and rapidly growing wealth of my generation as we lived the postwar boom years. Add to the mix that he was an inventive engineer, whereas I was a student of literature and then theology, and there were plenty of grounds for reasonably amicable but mutual confusions.

My mother came from a humbler background, first in rural Bedfordshire and then in the Midlands, and was brought up Methodist and nonconformist in other senses too—her father, who sold soap around the coalmines of the East Midlands, was deeply suspicious of anything establishment. Politically she was liberal left while my father was soft-hearted right. As her circumstances improved along with that of many others in postwar Britain, she welcomed and enjoyed all that rising living standards brought. By nature highly gregarious and practical, she gladly took on the traditional role of homemaker, mother, and wife to a successful engineer. She seemed to have few questions about generously enjoying the rapidly growing prosperity that the Harold Macmillan ("You have never had it so good") years brought to people in the Birmingham suburbs, which her Warwickshire village rapidly became. Celebration and austerity, the care of self and the needs of others, generosity of spirit and frugality, spending and careful stewardship, these were the poles of endless family discussion and complicated financial decisions. It did not make for a particularly integrated idea of how to make my own lifestyle choices.

I was brought up with the typical British public-school attitudes of self-reliance and independence. So I had little sympathy for those who might be needy; within my small world it all made sense that hard work brought rewards. Each holiday from the age of fourteen I took jobs ranging from building roof-trusses in the local wood yard to being an orderly on a surgical ward of Birmingham Accident Hospital until, in the interests of fostering those self-reliant qualities, I went off to Thailand for much of the year before university. During those months, particularly on the long overland trek back home at the end of the year through countries such as India and Afghanistan, I encountered serious poverty and a wider world. So began some years of attempting to live in a fuller awareness of those realities and with as few possessions as possible—while, contradictorily, enjoying the extreme privileges afforded to a student at Cambridge. With hindsight it is easy enough to see that very little of this made much theological or logical sense, but there is a reason why the prayer "forgive the sins of my youth" is in the Psalms. It was confusing certainly, but at least some enduring friendships have survived those years, so there is plenty of cause for gratitude. It seems that a wide variety of ways of living with our privileges has emerged over the years that have followed, so vivid discussions continue.

The week before we both left Cambridge, one of those friendships became particularly enduring when Miranda agreed to marry me. Many of the practical decisions we faced in the months that followed took us into a quite different level of involvement with money and possessions. Before too long, we were trying to bring two reasonably disparate sets of values and attitudes about money to bear on the choices we were making in our home and in providing for a growing family. Miranda shared my commitments to what we understood as radical Christian living, the wider world church, and the probability of a cross-cultural life. Her father had taught in Uganda for four years, and she was well aware of how life was lived outside of the UK from time spent with her family there, as well as from two years spent living in France. But by nature she is an artist with an intensely lived response to beauty and she is easily provoked to gratitude. So the grimmer and more dutiful views of a husband tempted to catastrophism, whether ecological or social, sat uncomfortably at times with her instincts for celebration and joy. The wonderful artist Mako Fujimura describes very clearly this dynamic within his own marriage:

One evening I sat alone, waiting for Judy to come home to our small apartment, worried about how we were going to afford the rent, to pay for the necessities over the weekend. Our refrigerator was empty and I had no cash left. Then Judy walked in with a bouquet of flowers. I got really upset. "How could you think of buying flowers if we can't even eat?" I remember saying, frustrated. Judy's reply has been etched on my heart for over thirty years now. "We need to feed our souls too." The irony is that I am an artist. I am the one, supposedly, feeding people's souls. But in worrying for tomorrow, in the stoic responsibility I felt to make ends meet, to survive, I failed to be the artist. Judy was the artist that day: she brought home the bouquet.[2]

At the time of writing, I am learning again how the global Christian creation care movement makes powerful common cause with an equal recovery of what Mako has called culture care. The contradictions and confusions of the Christian church in many parts of the world about the value of the material world, whether God's direct handiwork or what we humanly create from and with it, afflict and baffle us all.

So, given many of the unresolved questions and unexamined attitudes (I fear these are known simply as prejudices) about money in early adult life, it is unsurprising that when I was finally propelled into fundraising, my unease only sharpened. Fundraising came into my life because, in order to do the work to which Miranda and I were sure, then as now, that we were called, it was necessary to begin an organization. No international Christian organization working in conservation existed at the time, and so starting one was the only option, as the missionary society to which by then we were already committed for work in East Africa made clear. When I wrote to them outlining our plans for a different project, a bird observatory and field study center in southern Europe, to my shame I said that I would do anything the project required except raise funds. The wise reply from John

Ball, their director, was the first wake-up call into a new world of understanding fundraising as ministry.

> I must say I was alarmed at you saying you want to have nothing to do with . . . the wider appeal to the Christian public. If you do not, who will? When the Lord, through the church in Kenya, called me to set up a Christian publishing house, I not only had to deal with the exciting things like ideas for books, talking to authors, and vision: I also had to deal with how to present the project to literature agencies, what capital we would need over five years, how we would become self-sufficient, as well as with very humdrum proof-reading! Surely if the Lord is giving you the vision for this, then you must be responsible to Him for thinking that through in practical terms because a Centre is a very practical matter.[3]

Our first experiences were rather dramatic and, although not unique, did not prove to be the norm for many subsequent years during which fundraising has played a major part in my working life. At the outset we decided there was already enough risk in the enterprise of setting up the world's first Christian bird observatory and field center without our forcing it into being. So we decided to tell no one what we needed to pay for the reconnaissance expedition to Portugal that would show us whether or not the project was viable. A few friends in our church were aware when we were going, but that was it. We booked air tickets with no money to pay for them and decided to tell the travel agents the story as we believed it would be a good one. In turn they decided to take the risk and humor us.

As the days passed, money began to arrive in extraordinary ways, one of the more memorable being the night when several houses in our road were broken into while an envelope containing a hundred pounds in ten-pound notes lay undisturbed in full view in our porch. We only discovered it in the morning. Late one afternoon, two months later, I returned from visiting the local hospital to hear that the travel agent had been on the phone to Miranda.

"Mrs. Harris, you will probably realize that despite these unusual circumstances, these tickets must be paid for by the end of the afternoon."

"You'll have your money," she said.

By then we were still seven hundred pounds short, and her calm account of the conversation was highly alarming. I could well imagine that the embittered travel agent might have good reason for seriously espousing atheism faced with such irresponsible Christian behavior. I also realized I had little clue of the penalties for obtaining air tickets under false pretenses: a week in Torremolinos perhaps? Was that why Benidorm was so crowded? Miranda's faith had been frightening, but the phone call from friends a few moments later to say that they had a thousand pounds to give us "for Portugal" was even more worrying. They knew nothing about our need to buy tickets but had recently become Christians and shortly afterwards had received a technical redundancy payment. They wanted it to be a gift of gratitude to God. So we paid the travel agent, who was suitably intrigued. We seemed to be straying into the dangerous world of the Christian paperback with the purple cover. I had never enjoyed books with titles like *Faith in the Fast Lane*, not least because we ourselves seemed to spend a fair amount of time on the hard shoulder.

It was as if we needed such unusually clear signals in the early years of the project because things were at times so difficult that anything less than certainty about what was going on would have cast us adrift. We were treated to a startling display of coincidences rather like a private fireworks display, all the more interesting because it was unexpected. We were not aware that we would come to appreciate it so much later on when we needed every ounce of conviction to overcome the difficulties that arose.

The running funds for A Rocha's[4] first three years came in response to a simple letter that we wrote with our first colleagues,

Les and Wendy Batty, to about eighty of our friends, in which we outlined the budget and asked for their support. None of them were wealthy, but many of them gave—and quite a few are still giving over thirty years later. We raised our own modest allowance from seven churches that had agreed to support us at the request of our missionary society, together with a top-up from their central funds—which in my memory were in turn heavily supported by legacies. But the real baptism into fundraising came when we identified a house called Cruzinha on a peninsula between two arms of an estuary. It was nothing less than ideal for the first A Rocha center, but we were faced with a capital sum to raise in a very short time as there was intense interest from other buyers. At the time, the amount the owners were asking, £80,000, seemed enormous, but we had always known this moment would come.

I am ashamed now of the way I badgered the Trustees to let me come back to England for two weeks and of the way I cornered friends and relations to give us ideas for people we could talk to about Cruzinha. My little set of photographs became gradually more dog-eared as they were produced several times each day, and I discovered it was customary on such ventures to have a smoothly laid-out colored leaflet with a persuasive text to leave with people. My parents and Kerry and Alan Ritchie allowed me to monopolize their phones, and Bob Pullan lent me his car so that I could get to four Merseyside churches in a morning.

It all generated far too much pressure for everyone concerned, but the problem was that we now cared about it too much to be cool and dispassionate. Very occasionally events become a little Technicolor as God heightens our perceptions to make things clearer than usual. During the two weeks in England, a pattern began to emerge, and I was frequently astonished as very unpromising conversations suddenly swung and people who had been showing only polite interest decided that after all they would support the project. It was clear that something was going on that was well out of my control, and after a while I began to enjoy the experience. I rapidly began to learn things about the surprising world of Christian funding, where it can be more important to spend a day with an elderly lady who can only give fifty pounds but who decides to pray, than half an hour with a wealthy man who might seem a more relevant person to talk to.

The wealthy Christians I met constantly surprised me. One or two lived very simply but administered hundreds of thousands of pounds, doing all they could to discover how God wished it to be spent. I had never appreciated what a difficult vocation it could be to enable Christian work by giving money away, and I became aware of how important it is to keep complete integrity where money is concerned. "Follow the money" was the advice given to Bob Woodward in the Watergate film *All the President's Men*, and it is a path that often leads to the truth about Christian organizations too.

Meanwhile I heard from Miranda that the chances of the house remaining unsold were daily becoming slimmer. The tenants had reached saturation point with so many people coming to see the house, and were refusing to show prospective buyers around anymore. My two weeks of traveling ended, and I returned to Portugal to await the outcome of the Trustees' meeting the following Saturday. With a final gift on the morning that they met to make the decision, the total was still five thousand pounds short. Their chairman was Bob Pullan, and his letter to me later recorded the outcome.

David Ager quietly said that what he thought the Lord had done was give us enough. So we phoned the owner . . . but he was out and we disbanded agreeing that David would phone Portugal later. He told me at about 10.30 pm that we had the house with no demurring from the owner. I had worked on the train home from the meeting and was suddenly transformed from a very weary middle-aged man to a renewed person. On Sunday morning there was a communion service and we told a few people as we went in but introduced it in our prayers for the congregation. I could see the happiness in the faces as I watched the A Rocha supporters coming down the aisle—others were similarly moved. It has been a wonderful thing for them to know what a great and faithful Lord we have and to know his very positive confirmation that Cruzinha is right. I do so wish you could have been there for I know a little of how you have suffered and felt frustrated over the past weeks. It is clear to me that this was the way to do it, for otherwise the involvement of so many others would have been much less. When I phoned the churches in the afternoon and late morning I had the same response of initial unbelief and then an outpouring of thanks and praise to God. I pray we can all be worthy of his trust in the future months and years to come.[5]

Of course none of us had the slightest idea then that the work at Cruzinha would be the seedbed for a global conservation movement.

With the wisdom of hindsight we should perhaps have set our sights even higher in two respects. We thought that purchasing the majority of the headland was entirely beyond us, but the price then was a tiny fraction of what its present owners seem to hope for. With more faith and ambition we could have saved ourselves decades of stress as illegal development proposals have continued to hang over the site ever since. Many subsequent years of time, effort, and money have gone into the research and legal action that have been needed to keep the ecological integrity of this special and important area. Maybe it could have been avoided—we will never know.

And, more modestly, we should have included the need for renovations and alterations to the building in the initial campaign to buy the property. It proved a far more protracted and difficult process to raise funds for this less dramatic although essential project than it had been to find the capital sum for the purchase.

Working around those shortages in the early years caused us all a great deal of practical and psychological stress, but I was learning two lessons.

First, it is precisely those needs that drive us into dependence on God and other people and so into a far wider and richer set of relationships. Because we had insufficient funds to buy what we needed, many other people were drawn into the work at Cruzinha and we became truly reliant on volunteer assistance. It made us more innovative and creative as we tackled the jobs without the normal conditions for getting them done. While volunteer efforts are rarely efficient if measured only by the time it takes to get work done, they are incomparably more personal than the commercial transactions we engage in when we solve problems by simply paying for new equipment or professional help.

Second, what speaks to those who wish to give is often a matter of the heart. The excitement and risk of securing Cruzinha, a beautiful rundown house ideally placed in the middle of an extraordinarily important natural landscape, made an immediate impact on those who heard about it, and people responded with great generosity. This seemed to be often against their better instincts, and certainly many were giving to an environmental project for the first time. This was the 1980s, remember. The mundane requirements of renovating, staffing, and equipping a bird observatory held no such appeal, so we had to wait for years to slowly build up the resources we needed. In consequence, a persistent uncertainty about whether the work was viable and sustainable was our daily companion.

Thankfully there was a growing income stream from those who stayed in the house, although the group we most wanted to be there, Portuguese students, were at a financial cost, not a benefit. In both these considerations lie two classic temptations for the fundraiser, both of which need to be clearly identified and resisted. The first is to dramatize the story beyond the truth—and even a cursory look at many fundraising campaigns reveals that to be a very common practice. The second is to push the organization away from its core vision and goals in order to achieve some kind of financial stability. Creativity in finding ways to fund the projects that we believe in is essential, and calm financial visibility brings many benefits, but if they come at the cost of losing the integrity of the enterprise, they are not worth it.

We were, however, able to find a way of making Cruzinha financially stable with many loyal supporters, a varied donor base, and a predictable income stream from a wide range of activities. After a decade of life at Cruzinha, we were finally in a position to fulfill the original objective of handing over the project to Portuguese leadership. We had been blessed with a number of highly gifted friends, many of them recent graduates, who had taken on the vision and made it their own. It was time to move on, and the unexpected number of requests that were coming from other parts of the world for us to help A Rocha get established elsewhere meant that there was plenty to do. It also brought us into contact for the first time with the enormous, baffling, and occasionally quite wealthy world of North American Christianity.

As we were soon looking for support for work in Africa, the Middle East, and South America, where local resources were often very limited, we naturally imagined this could be a marriage made in heaven. It was a rude awakening to discover that many Christian churches we visited, and Christian foundations we talked to, believed that environmental work was essentially political, and certainly of no significance to anything Christians would think important. It was equally alarming to find, not only that were there very few Christians working in environmental organizations, but that the typical narrative was that Christian thinking and practice were the prime culprits for environmental degradation, historically but also now.[6] Big corporations were also blamed, but a perception I frequently encountered in the conservation world was summarized by one of its more prominent leaders, who told me that in his view "evangelical theology and unrestrained corporate behavior" were the two greatest threats to global biodiversity, and that they frequently overlapped in the person of their leaders. He backed up his convictions by giving us significant funding to try to bring churches located in areas where biodiversity is concentrated to a more biblical view of creation care. We are still hoping for the resources we need to do more to persuade Christian corporate leaders to align their business and investment decisions with the biblical wisdom that would protect vulnerable species and habitats.

And so we met with a striking and almost complete lack of financial success, apart from a few startling and very helpful exceptions. The sheer hard work of gaining and keeping foundation grants, the jet-lagged travel for meetings, the paperwork, the reporting, the huge need for clarity as donor expectations and field realities clashed and re-formed, all was a new world to this particular intuitive, detail-averse, arts grad pastor. I loved the new people I was meeting and the new places I visited. Vancouver! New York! California! Grand Rapids! Washington, DC! But then there were months and years of follow-up, pounding the keys of a computer on trains, buses, and planes or back in Les Tourades, the new A Rocha center in France.

Worst of all was simply trying to get answers to questions both from my new A Rocha colleagues in inaccessible places and my new foundation friends who had now moved on to the next thing in their busy urban lives. Incidentally, it was a challenge trying to make calls and write proposals in a center where we froze in winter and boiled in summer. Even though it was the second time around as we set up the new center in France, I was unable once again to find sufficient support to set up adequate running budgets. This time, too, we relied heavily on volunteer help, but it brought a great amount of strain and delay to all involved. There were of course great relational gains, but I obviously had not learned the lessons of Cruzinha. That was even harder to understand when the money to buy and partially equip the house came as the most astonishing start-up gift in A Rocha's history to that point, contradicting all I had by now come to believe about how reasonable fundraising went forward. It simply defied explanation and was completely transformative for our work—but that is another story. I am consoled that other A Rocha leaders in their subsequent journeys have encountered similar paradoxes.[7]

In time, it was possible to recruit more experienced help for the technical fundraising that increasingly occupied us, and again my needs and inabilities proved the way by which many others joined our team and became valued friends and colleagues. It was becoming clearer that my own gifts lay in enthusing and inspiring people, and not organizations, to support A Rocha in many different ways. It was in thinking of the friends I had who possessed the means to help A Rocha at the new level of giving that was needed for a growing organization that I came across the greatest gain that fundraising brought into my life. As with so much in the area of fundraising, it was paradoxical.

I might have imagined that, through practice and what was now turning into years of effort and literally hundreds of proposals and campaigns, I would have developed a kind of expertise and ability, and so a greater rate of financial success. There is no doubt that I improved at a technical level and at least did not make as many of my early mistakes, such as omitting critical information and not listening to what the donor cared about in my eagerness to explain what we were doing and why it would change the world. Or a couple of acres in Lima anyway . . . But this expertise was of no help in combatting the true condition of the person who seeks funds from other people. I do not mean the fundraiser who is working through a technical program of activities with donor organizations, but my kind of fundraiser, the one who likes people.

Most medium-sized nonprofits will tell you that, despite their best intentions, much of their funding comes from a very few people rather than the broad-based, calm raft of donor organizations that would be their preferred support base. One obvious reason for this is that most foundations limit their engagement to a certain number of years for fear that their recipients will become dependent on them. They understand that financial comfort stifles innovation (the mantra from business is that if you wish to destroy an organization, overcapitalize it), and so their support never lasts very long. Personal donors, however, will typically know your work quite well and be closely involved, so they are aware of how things are going and can judge their contributions. Thus, over time, unless the nonprofit is really large and has developed a kind of business plan with a steady income stream from somewhere, the percentage of support from individual contributions tends to rise.

Fundraisers like me, whose work is primarily personal, may know what I mean when I say that the essential condition of the fundraiser is vulnerability. There are good and bad reasons for that. The bad reason is that, despite the clear teaching of Jesus (Mark 12:41-44) and the early church (James 2:1-4) that we should not measure people according to their financial means, we Christians do. It is so hard to resist the signals that large houses and cars or imposing offices can give. A strange social dynamic can develop for both donor and asker. It tends to produce a certain defensiveness on the part of wealthy Christians for having what they do, and it frequently gives a sense of inadequacy and failure to people seeking support because they are clearly, in some way, less "successful" or why would they need help? I found, time and again, that these issues, both for me and for potential donors, were expressed in subtle but significant ways. It wasn't easy for people to turn me down, and so evasion became the tactic. Many wealthy people live complicated lives across many places, and so the gaps become their refuge. As for me, I found I could be kept waiting, or would have meetings canceled at short notice, even after I had journeyed long distances to be there. The most difficult thing of all was that communications could simply cease with no explanation, or that, even after we had been encouraged to apply for a particular kind of work, when all was prepared and we went to the next stage, then the rules and interests would suddenly have changed.

In the case of the foundations, this was because the staff themselves had difficulty discerning the intentions of the donor. If the donor had died this was even more problematic, and, ironically, it could be so in two opposite ways. A good example of the first is the case of Henry Ford, who had not explained at all how he wanted his major bequest to be used, which created well-documented internal power struggles among those who were then tasked with applying the funds. However, if the deceased donor's intentions were too definite, then it could be hard for the foundation staff to translate them into fundable work that was needed in the world they now lived in. Both of these problems were easily exported with even greater force to those who came seeking grants.

On the other hand, we have been blessed in those staff who stayed many years with a foundation or who worked long-term for a donor, and their willingness to really understand our work, and then to advocate for us, was a real gift. Very often they became friends, and that friendship went far beyond the merely professional. We sought to honor them all, at every level of the organizations we engaged with, and to validate their crucial roles.

For some years I fought, in good and bad ways, the vulnerability that is a necessary condition of the fundraiser. The good ways were, perhaps, in working to improve my technical skills and in recruiting those who were certainly better at parts of the fundraising process than I was. The bad ways—such as justifying my attitudes of resentment or envy, or feeling critical of wealth itself, although we depended on our wealthier friends for A Rocha's support—were as bad as they sound. I, and no doubt some of my friends, realized I had a problem, but it came to a head when I got into a short-tempered exchange with a new potential donor. After we had talked together about A Rocha's work for just over ten minutes, he knew, because his business bets had worked, how his analysis of what we were doing would solve all our problems. My overreaction showed my colleagues (and later, somewhat reluctantly, me!) that I had begun to lose the plot. I had fallen into believing that money and the different kinds of power it gave really did matter more than anything else for A Rocha's well-being and so for my own. I had begun to assume that if A Rocha had more money we would do better work. And I had begun to resent the lives and experiences of the wealthy and to think my own noble life and experience were more valuable.

I knew, from the helpful guidance of a colleague who had worked in fundraising for many years, that it was my job to discover what the donor cared about and to see if it matched what we wanted to do. My colleague had explained that it was generally useless to try to persuade a donor to see the world your way and to care that, in his favorite example, the roof of A Rocha's center in Lebanon was leaking. People give their money away to change the world in the ways they think important, just as those of us who work in the nonprofit world, typically at some cost of different kinds, do the same. We may give less money and more time and energy, but all of us give and receive. The only question is whether we care about the same things, and if the resources of the one can find an appropriate way of meeting the needs of the other. But the relationships that lie at the heart of developing that growing understanding are even more important.

Furthermore, as we've explained in the biblical section, the primary relationship for any Christian is the one with God in Christ, and I think those of us who try to raise funds in his name meet him most powerfully as we understand the meaning of Jesus's own vulnerability. In order to obey the Father, Jesus and later his followers "lost all things" (Phil. 3:8). They were very clear about what they were called to be and to do, as we also need to be. This clarity and growing discernment of our identity and calling are critical for any fundraising effort. That is what will give the passion to our appeal—these are not just our bright ideas we are sharing. We do believe we have understood something of the purposes of God, however small and however local. And then we ourselves are committed to paying a price, just as we are asking the people we wish to support us to do by contributing their money.

So I have found that the real question, the deeper discussion, both for me and for A Rocha, is what God is wanting of us. The question of how, and when, his purposes will be realized is secondary. It is always our aim that the relationships within A Rocha, and with those who support us, should be characterized by trust. If those involved are Christians, it will be a shared trust in God who makes all things possible according to what he wants. If they are not, then they can still bear the fruits of a trust that allows us to be honest, vulnerable, and deeply authentic as we present our needs to someone who is materially far more privileged than we are.

It can get more complex than these short paragraphs convey. Friends become donors and donors become friends. Our conversations have many layers, and over years our circumstances can change dramatically. It was Rod who taught me how to do some disentangling by being far more straightforward. "Just say to the friend you hope might support you, 'Can I talk to you about money?'" he told me during one of our first sessions of sharing experiences in philanthropy. "If they say 'yes,' they have taken the responsibility for what follows and you can relax. If they say 'no, I would rather not' or 'this isn't a good time,' then you know where you are and you can continue in friendship without being embarrassed." I still find it difficult, because many of us Brits are, as I explained, as conflicted and complicated about money as we are about many other things, but I am improving. As a college friend once wrote in a different context, "Once I was blind but now I am short-sighted." On most days, I will settle for that.

Once we become familiar with the idea that fundraising is best seen as a form of ministry like any other, then of course many insights from Scripture, and from the older and wiser Christian writers who inspire or train us, find their natural application in fundraising. We simply need to gain the habit of expecting their wisdom, just as we do when we consider the more mainstream topics of worship, evangelism, preaching, or prayer.

As friends and as writers, both John Stott and Eugene Peterson have had a profound influence on my approach to fundraising as well as my wider Christian thinking. More recently, Ellen Davis's wonderful work on the book of Proverbs has resonated deeply with what I have been learning over the years about fundraising wisely. One reason for that is her interest in both culture and agriculture, and each one holds appropriate metaphors for understanding fundraising in a biblical way. Industrial or economic metaphors are, by contrast, much less suitable, although with their insistence on numbers and metrics they now dominate popular Christian thinking whenever growth is in question.

The book of Proverbs constantly offers wisdom for the most practical aspects of life, not least money and status, and it is therefore of particular relevance to all who would fundraise in a godly fashion. So I have been trying to get used to applying the texts, greatly helped by Ellen Davis's commentary, to this related and particular area of human fruitfulness. Let me give an example.

When commenting on the introduction to the Proverbs, where we read that these writings are for "gaining instruction in wise dealing, righteousness, justice and equity" (Prov. 1:2-3, NRSV), Ellen Davis writes:

> The Bible is not interested in abstract knowledge—that is, in knowledge abstracted from goodness. It is not interested in knowledge abstracted from the concrete problem of how to live well with our neighbors, in the presence of God.[8]

She applies her conclusions to education as power, as opposed to education for the common good, but they are also clearly relevant to how much importance we may be tempted to give to technique, or to abstract expertise, in fundraising. They are even more pertinent to how we might be tempted to think competitively of ourselves as fundraisers. Proverbs' understanding that God's wisdom, rather than our ambitions or supposed strengths, should govern all our relationships can make many passages directly relevant to fundraisers who are wondering where new resources will come from or feeling under pressure. Here is just one that reorients our understanding of fruitfulness within creation and reestablishes our foundations as we endeavor to work well in God's world.

> By wisdom the Lord laid the earth's foundations;
>   by understanding he set the heavens in place;
> by his knowledge the watery depths were divided,
>   and the clouds let drop the dew. (Prov. 3:19-20)

Another of Ellen Davis's insights about the land and how it was watered and became fruitful was very helpful to me personally as I tried to work out whether the normal condition for a Christian organization like A Rocha was likely to be prosperity or scarcity. Our finances had typically been fairly precarious over the years, but unusually we were in a season of relative financial security when I read what she wrote from an agrarian perspective on what God's ways meant for God's people in the paradigmatic story of the Exodus.[9]

In summary, it was when the children of Israel were in Egyptian slavery that they benefited from the Pharaoh's exercise of money, power, and wisdom. Even slaves within the "industrial-military complex" had access to the seasonal conditions of the Nile floods that annually brought water, exactly when it was needed, to be harnessed by a high-tech irrigation system. Water was readily available for watering crops there, unlike neighboring regions. "The land you are entering to take over is not like the land of Egypt, from which you have come, where you planted your seed and irrigated it by foot as in a vegetable garden" (Deut. 11:10).

By contrast to Egypt, where the children of Israel were slaves, God's Promised Land certainly "flowed with milk and honey," but only when the strip of semi-arid hills between the "desert" of the Mediterranean and the true desert to the east received rain. That was never certain; it was always bound up with the way the people of God were living in relationship with their Creator within a covenant that encompassed the creation itself (Deuteronomy 32).

Davis points out that, just as "agriculture has an ineluctably ethical dimension,"[10] so it was for the survival and flourishing of the children of Israel; a precarious existence was intrinsic to the very nature of the Promised Land. The way through the wilderness, characterized by God's outrageous provision of manna and of water from rocks, was the preparation for the faithful life that would be necessary to thrive under such theocentric conditions.

As I reflected upon our fundraising work within A Rocha, I realized that perhaps it was through living precariously that we would learn more of God's character. We were not intended to be powerful and impressive; we were intended to be an organization that recognized how dependent we were on God's provision. That in turn would come through right discernment of his intentions for us, through people's generosity, and through our faithful vulnerability as we worked for funds. It was in that kind of cultivation that deeply trusting and rooted relationships with God, each other, and the creation could truly grow.

CHAPTER 11

Rod's Story

1. What has been the nature of your involvement in fundraising?

As Christians, my wife Bev and I have long believed that it is incumbent on us to do at least three things with our money. I am not offering these in a proselytizing spirit nor as a prescription for anyone. And while I am not providing the rationale behind each of these decisions in this context, they do let the reader know our fundamental perspective on giving. First, we believe that giving away 15 percent of our net income is an important spiritual discipline. Second, we believe that some of that money should be given to individuals or organizations who are unable to provide a tax receipt. Third, we believe that if we are working in a nonprofit environment, a significant portion of our financial giving should go to that organization. These experiences of giving financially over many years have had a strong influence on our understanding of philanthropy.

While I have raised money from those who would not identify as Christian, all of my fundraising has been for projects that were associated with Christian causes. As President of a theological institution, I was responsible, in concert with the Board of

Governors, for ensuring that the fundraising team raised funds in a way that reflected the ethos and mission of the institution and met annual financial targets. It was expected that I would do fundraising as a key part of my presidential work, particularly in relationship with those who had higher capacity to give, as well as overseeing campaigns or special fundraising projects.

As a pastor in a couple of different churches, I was involved in various projects where funds were required either for special projects or for annual expenses. A core responsibility was determining how much was needed, how it should be raised, and how we would know when funds had reached a place where we could confidently move ahead with a specific focus.

As Vice-President and Academic Dean of another theological institution, I was part of a team that prepared budgets and ascertained how much was needed from tuition, donations, ancillary expenses, and residence fees. These multi-pronged financial decisions then led to a particular directive being given to the person overseeing fundraising for the school so people could be solicited for specific amounts of money.

As a board member in various organizations, I had fiduciary and missional responsibility to ensure that I was bringing wisdom, wealth, and work to the table. In nonprofit contexts this meant not only overseeing budgets and development targets but also participating in the evaluation of fundraising methods and targets and being an exemplar of the organization by giving financially myself.

As a consultant, I have interacted with many individuals, churches, and organizations who have sought help on various aspects of fundraising, whether it was staffing, structure, methods, targets, marketing, or donor relations. Many of these consulting experiences have helped me clarify and understand the work of philanthropy in more detail and have also allowed me to learn from the successes and failures of others.

How has all this impacted my approach to fundraising? The

fact that I have listed being a Christian before being a president, pastor, vice president, academic dean, board member, and consultant is significant. While there is a field of fundraising, a growing professionalization within that field, more and more consultants, and a proliferation of books, articles, and websites, the hard learning and embodiment of philanthropy in my own life may be the most important aspect of my understanding of fundraising. How can I help others to give if I have not gone through the process myself? How can I request funds from others if I have not made the hard decisions that have led to my own giving? How can I invite others to sacrifice if I do not manifest the same spirit with my money? If those who raise money have not had the experience of what it is like to give money, I wonder whether they can enter into the fundraising transaction with integrity and empathy.

This point extends to those who are members of communities where funds are being raised. If a Board of Governors agrees on a particular direction for the organism, does it not follow that they will also give financially if they are able to do so? How can fundraisers ask those outside the institution to give funds if those inside have not exhibited a sacrificial spirit to do the same? I have been interested to hear some donors question the viability of a given project if it appears that those on the "inside" have not demonstrated their own support. In many cases the "inside" and "outside" giving will not be in equal amounts, but equal sacrifice adds a lot to the integrity of the external request.

I am conscious that, unlike Peter, my various roles have not included raising money for my own salary or expenses. Many organizations utilize this method, and while the overall principles in this book apply in that situation, it is a form of philanthropy that I have found to be complicated. How do I ask for my own salary? How will people read that amount? Does this make fundraising appear self-serving? When I was in pastoral ministry, any proposed talk or sermon on philanthropy stimulated discussion among the leadership about whether I should do it and run the risk of appearing to be self-serving, or whether someone else should do it and keep it removed from anything to do with me or my role.

In my roles as a pastor, vice president, academic dean, and consultant, I was not accountable for how much money came in via fundraising, and it was not a critical success factor for my performance. Pastors are not typically assessed using this means; nor are academic administrators or consultants. In contrast, CEOs are held to a different standard. High-quality boards who hold the ultimate power and authority in the profit and not-for-profit world will systematically evaluate their CEO to determine whether the what, how, and why of fundraising are being done well, will hold the institution responsible for its fundraising, and will participate actively in fundraising themselves. Disengaged boards will only use dollars raised as the key metric, failing to realize the larger issues embodied within truly Christian philanthropy.

Presidents of nonprofits are usually responsible to a board for everything that happens in an institution. In healthy situations, three things usually facilitate successful fundraising in the presidential role. First, the president and board work in tandem, with clear and direct communication along with an open understanding of the issues, direction, and critical success factors. Second, the core ministry is effective, in tune with contemporary realities, and staffed with high-quality people who have attitudes and skills that facilitate the flourishing of the mission with a view to impacting the world beyond the institution. And third, there are people in the constituency who understand the institution, value its mission, and believe that it is having an impact in a way that is in step with the contemporary culture. When all three of these facets of the institution are in place, under the oversight of the president, fundraising is a joy even though the president bears the burden of achieving fundraising targets and making institutional budgets, both of which are central to the overall well-being of the institution.

Presidents, CEOs, executive directors, and other senior leaders are always in an unenviable dance with the potentially competing demands of mission, marketing, and money. Mission is typically understood by the answer we give to questions about how the world is impacted by what we do; marketing is what we tell people about the impact we are having on the world; and as we think of money we ask how the financial resources we gather will impact the world through what they make possible. In a mature organization, there are clear and compelling responses to all three of these areas and the linkage between them is coherent. When the leader goes to donors to ask for money, she is not asking for money simply to support what is being done, nor will it be essential to have a slick but disconnected marketing campaign to tell the story. Organizations that move in that direction can expect a less-than-engaged philanthropic community and lots of internal strife about why more funds are not coming in, why fundraisers are not successful, and why donors seem less than interested in the great things the organization is doing. While a community may be enthralled with what they are doing, it is vital that they understand that donors are constantly making hard choices between innumerable calls on their giving. As one of my friends told me, "Donors do not give to internally verified worthy cause thinking." Donors do not give to good intent or what is being done. They give to impact and influence.

This is why executive directors who want to be good fundraisers require "impact thinkers" in the management of their mission and their marketing. If the core of the organization centers around what we are doing, how we think we are doing, and how well we are being treated, valued, and paid for what we are doing, then fundraising will be a challenge because the mission lacks an outward perspective and is inwardly focused. However, if the front-line staff and their leaders are in tune with the culture, have a clear sense of global realities, know what is required to actually impact those realities, and act on that knowledge to achieve the desired impact, then it will be far easier to find funds to support the work. For example, as I have observed different ministries over the past few decades, it is not a surprise that those with a focused social-justice agenda seem to be doing well attracting donors. Contemporary concern over justice issues, intensified by the expansion of media and Internet coverage and combined with a greater global sensibility, have led more people to ask how their funds can be used to bring justice throughout the world.

Along with an outward missional focus, a clear external trajectory on marketing is also central for effective fundraising. If "what we say about ourselves" is more tied to the experience of "those within" than to "those without," we run the risk of giving potential donors the message that "we are impressed with what we are doing and we would like you to be impressed as well, so much so that you will give us money." While there is a temptation to tell the world about "us," our organization, our employees, our leadership, and our work, we need to realize that there are a massive number of other organizations telling the same story about how wonderful they are. Many donors have become weary of fundraisers who are simply advocating for their organization rather than inviting people into a relationship that will impact the world for good and for God. Increasingly, donated money is finding its way to organizations with an outward focus in both mission and marketing, and executive directors who ignore this reality do so at their own peril and that of the organization. In fact, their overall success may be dependent on their ability to help the organization be outwardly focused, to see each of the parts working together as a whole, and to demonstrate the organization's commitment to a mission and marketing trajectory that minimizes intent and prizes impact.

2. What is your personal story on money, wealth, and fundraising?

While theology—faith that seeks understanding about God—is central to the life of the Christian, if we fail to understand the powerful importance of biography it is a denial of our humanity as those created in the image of God. Understanding God's story in creation, in Scripture, in history and tradition, as well as in the contemporary world often requires an understanding of our own stories. Where have I come from? What have I learned? What have I been exposed to? What values have been given to me? Where does my story merge with God's story or depart from it? When it comes to the subject of money and fundraising, it is often in the interaction of my story and God's story that I learn, grow and mature, and have a wiser perspective. And this is just my story, my experience, not that of my parents, brother, or sister. The four of them, coming from different vantage points, may describe their experience very differently.

It is important that fundraisers have not just a clear understanding of the biblical, theological, conceptual, and practical dimensions of philanthropy but also have familiarity with their own history and the ability to articulate its influence with a degree of self-knowledge.

My parents moved with me, their four-year-old son, from Dublin, Ireland, to Canada in 1956. As my mother often told me, they "came here with nothing," which I always interpreted, accurately or inaccurately, as a financial statement that often graces the lips of immigrants. I assumed they must have saved up all they had, spent it on the costs of immigration, and started fresh in the new world. We lived in very modest accommodations in my early years, and although there was no detailed conversation about it, I assumed they had very little. Over time they had two more children, a boy and a girl, and were able to purchase a home, and a second car, and I started to realize that, while we were far from rich, we were the classic middle-income family with enough funds to pay the bills and have an annual holiday, but with little left for extravagance of any sort. Later in life I sensed that my parents had more financial stability, and like many immigrants this became for them a point of emphasis, even pleasure, because "we came here with nothing."

They had come from a Christian background in Ireland where they had been connected with the Open Plymouth Brethren movement. When we moved to Canada, for various reasons, they ended up in a much more rigid and conservative branch of Brethrenism. As is true of many sectarian movements, one of the driving principles in our local assembly was a particular interpretation of Paul's statement as rendered by the King James Version of 2 Corinthians 6:17–"come out from among them and be ye separate." Brethren had their origins in the 1820s in Ireland where a number of disaffected laypeople and clergy left the Church of Ireland and started a movement that eventually grew during the century that followed into a formidable force. In fact, they acquired their nickname "Plymouth Brethren" because their church in Plymouth, England, had over a thousand people. The Brethren transition from the mainline church to this new expression of the body of Christ was a "coming out" and a "being separate," but that mantra applied to everything.

As a young child I remember hearing sermons, and sitting in Bible studies, where two standards were held up. We were not to be like "the world," which included everything that was linked with contemporary culture, and we were to avoid the "sects and systems," which included all other denominations and expressions of faith, be they Protestant or Roman Catholic. "Coming out and being separate" was the reactive identity that pervaded that body, with considerable emphasis on what not to be or do and much less concern about how to live and function in a pluralistic world with multiple religions. The world and the church were suspect, could not be trusted, and piety was achieved by the avoidance of both. Identity was formed via negation.

This approach colored the topic of money and anything related to it. Churches paid pastors, but we did not. Worldly people loved their money, but we did not. Wealthy people in our church were seen as a little less spiritual than the rest of us. Fundraising both in the church and in the world was done publicly, but we did not do that. I remember as a child hearing about the consternation of the leadership when the government brought in tax receipts for church donations. To buy into such a practice was to let the "left hand know what the right hand was doing," and it was an accounting system from the world. Preachers and missionaries were brought in from various parts of the world and were often described as not "on salary like the sects and systems" but living "by faith." And because the King James Version was the appropriate version of Scripture for our little assembly of believers, the term "fellowship" was used as a code word for money. Even in our annual general meeting where the finances were discussed, it was called the Fellowship Tea, and you would never hear the term "money" mentioned once. In fact, all my memories about money in that context are linked with "filthy lucre," the KJV translation of various New Testament passages (1 Tim. 3:3, 8; Titus 1:7, 11; 1 Pet. 5:2), along with "fellowship," a term that was seen as synonymous with money (2 Cor. 8:4; Gal. 2:9; Phil. 1:5).

Our church buildings were spartan and lacking in any aesthetic value, reflecting again the perception that other denominations spent money excessively on "things seen" but we did not. However, a number of people in our church were well off financially, had a nice cottage on a lake, took elaborate holidays, and often had beautiful and well-furnished homes with high-end cars. For me, the fact that money was neither mentioned nor utilized when we were worshiping in the church building reinforced a subtle lack of integration. Our church expression of Christian faith did not require money, but our private tastes and aspirations were in a different category. We were able to live comfortably with a simple church building and spiritual life along with a nicely endowed house and expensive car.

While we did not use the term "theology" in our church and preferred to see ourselves as Bible-believing Christians, there was a clear dualism in how we understood earth and heaven, material and spiritual, world and Christian, along with other supposed dichotomies. With well-selected proof texts we would argue that the earth was passing away, the material was irrelevant because it would experience the same fate, and the world was a suspicious place that was not at all an appropriate home for the Christian. As a result evangelism was centered on "getting out of here and going there," sanctification was about getting your inner life moving in the right direction, and the appropriate aspiration for life was to flee the material and pursue the spiritual. Any notions of seeing the spiritual in the material, or living Christianly by being good stewards of creation, were not present, with the result that money did not seem to have the capacity to come under the Lordship of Christ or be used for good, here and now, on the earth. We were most guided by the fact that you could not take it with you when you went to the other side.

Another interesting wrinkle in the church dualism was the use of the term "business." Business was linked with money, the corporate world, reality, a contrast to the church and spirituality, and another synonym for money. The men, and it was always that gender, who were in business were in the "real world," knew how to handle money, and could be trusted with all financial matters, and if their "secular" work was in the financial realm then they were considered to have competence in all things money. Men who were doctors, mechanics, or teachers could have significant biblical understanding, theological expertise, and winsome spirituality, but they were not considered to have the requisite skills to deal with this earthly, materialistic form of exchange. "That is not the way we do it in business" was a common critique of regular

Christians trying to bring a spiritual grid to the financial matters of the church.

When I was eleven years old I delivered TV Guides door to door in the apartment where we lived. With twenty subscribers on my list, I received four cents for each guide that I sold, resulting in a weekly influx of cash to the amount of eighty cents! While a meager amount by contemporary standards, this was a lot for a young boy in 1963, and I well recall the sense of power, control, and status that came from amassing that kind of wealth.

At the time, my parents instilled two values in me that had practical and long-term outcomes. First, money was to be saved so that you could spend it at a later date and not have to go into debt. Impulsive spending was frowned upon, as was spending if you had no money, and money in the present was always framed in light of the future. What might you be able to do with what you had saved? How might you be able to delay gratification? Could you retain the money for a greater purpose? Frivolous utilization of money was highly suspect, and while I would not describe my parents as frugal, they held being intentional with money as a high value. So when I paid cash for my first plug-in radio in 1964 for a little less than twenty dollars, there was not just enjoyment for me in being able to listen to my favorite music, sports, and phone-in shows, but there was also a sense of "well done" in the family and pleasure that I made the purchase without debt. The money had been hard earned, saved well, and was now being used to purchase a valuable commodity without incurring extra cost. The "pride of ownership" gripped me and my parents.

Interestingly, my parents were not oriented to things and could not be described as living lavishly or materialistically. My father was an engineer in government working for the Ministry of Environment with an emphasis on water treatment, while my mother did what many women started to do in the 1960s, full-time home-making and parenting along with various part-time jobs. I never knew how much they made, but saving was important and you needed to be "careful" with spending. I have many memories of my parents using the "careful" word around money, and I knew how to translate it. Do not spend quickly. Do not spend unless you can afford it. Do not go into debt. My parents would frequently talk about saving for their retirement as a way to not spend in the moment, and that became an infrequent apologetic when I would ask them for something. Sadly, my father passed away shortly after his retirement, and in spite of their shared expectations my mother did not have the enjoyment of spending their saved money with him.

My parents also taught me that the entire eighty cents from the TV Guide route did not belong exclusively to me. As I grew up in a Christian home, my parents explained that I should set aside 10 percent of my earnings to give to the church or other worthy causes. While I do not remember what causes grabbed my attention, I learned that taking 10 percent of your income and ensuring that money went elsewhere was righteous and right. In later years Bev and I moved that percentage to 15 and have continued with that pattern to the present. I do not recall direct teaching on how to approach the other 90 or 85 percent, but while my parents never talked about their own income or their own tithing, they established a holy habit in me that has persisted to this day. It is inconceivable to have income without setting a designated portion aside, whether I perceive the overall income to be extensive or not.

Over the years I have had a few people respond to this part of my story by accusing me of being legalistic, living oppressively under some nebulous standard. Why 10 percent? Why 15 percent? Why not 20 percent? Why put a percentage on it at all? Is it from gross earnings or net earnings? However, I have never experienced this percentage as legalistic in the sense of it being oppressive. For me it has been what the Puritans would call a "holy habit," doing the right thing because it is the right thing to do. It is not an oppressive influence from something outside. It is delight from something inside. It is not burdensome and obligatory, but I do

students in the program would make more at the commencement of our careers than he was making at the end of his professional life. In the 1970s the link between education and high salaries was quite linear, so one could expect that high-quality training would lead to an excellent salary. Many of us got on that track in attitude and aspiration, believing that our education was a ticket to something bigger and better and that money would be at the center.

Immersed in the heady allure of that hope, Bev and I began to sense even before we were married that our call in life was not to make money and become wealthy but to provide services and help to people who might not be able to afford it under normal circumstances. It was not long after we were married that I found myself in a job interview in an office of a local Bible college. "Found myself" is the right phrase because I had no interest in working in Christian theological education, largely because I saw it as a conceptualization and professionalization of a faith that was inherently spiritual and embodied. More than that, it seemed removed from the real world, and its holy huddle ethos did not appeal to me in the least. Now, looking back, I realize that this new job was not due to personal choice but more to God's providence. It became the beginning of a career path where money was not a goal but a by-product of something much more significant—serving and ministering to others.

I remember trying to explain to my secular employer, who was providing this in-training young psychologist with an excellent paycheck, why I wanted to leave and work in a Bible college. Fortunately I did not tell her my new salary, but had she known that figure she would have reacted even more strongly than she did. Why would I give up a professional trajectory in the secular world? Why would I move into a field that lacked unlimited advancement and financial growth? Why did I not realize that a subsequent master's degree in theology would do nothing to help my climb into socioeconomic freedom? My current theological paradigm sees the kingdom of God permeating both the so-called secular and sacred worlds, but in the late 1970s that job change from the former to the latter was an implicit acknowledgment that there had to be other things than making a lot of money and climbing a professional ladder. I learned then, as I have learned many times since, that whatever your station in life, money has to be put in some sort of perspective. Our approach to money, much more than the amount of it, says a lot about who we are and how much we are willing to sacrifice. If I tell you how much time I spend thinking and talking about money, you will probably have deep insight into who I am. The objects of our worship tell us a lot about the worshipers.

Now in my seventh decade, I am at the stage where the explicit and implicit messages about money are even more intense. I look back on my life as a psychologist, pastor, professor, and administrator and ask many questions. Did I make career choices that allowed me to live in luxury for my closing days? Do I have enough for retirement? What is enough? Can I retain my current lifestyle? Do I want to? Am I entitled to a certain way of living because of what I have done in my life? How do I cope with the volatility of the stock market and real estate worlds? The appetizing and captivating side of money raises its head again, and many people in my age group turn this important aspect of life into its core aspect. Money, how much I have, what I will have, the nature of retirement, become central, and all becomes entangled with presumption, entitlement, fear, anxiety, and angst, often with a significant lack of faith in the God who provides. When such a mindset dominates, it is easy to forget giving and sacrificing money for the common good and to replace it with subtle hoarding and the pride of ownership. Maybe you "can't take it with you," but it would sure be nice to have a lot in the season before you go. Through many years of fundraising I have wondered if sizeable wealth toward the end of life, whether in cash, real estate, or things, is any guarantee of a life of peaceful tranquility, quiet godliness, and open relationships, and in my more lucid moments I have noted that many people who have less, frequently have more.

3. What has it been like for you to be a fundraiser?

Three words describe my experience as a fundraiser—*reluctance, joy,* and *angst.*

Reluctance

One of the shared experiences that have drawn Peter and me together is that we both would describe our journey to fundraising as reluctant. When we first met in the early 2000s, we both had worked in Christian organizations and churches, and we realized that in our early years we had a mental struggle and disinclination as we sought to raise funds. However, being reluctant to drive the fourteen hours straight through to get to your holiday destination is not a statement on your dislike of driving or your aversion to the place where you are going. It is more a time of pause as you weigh up whether you should break up the journey or get up very early to depart, or whether there is benefit in arriving one day late. So reluctance has the potential to be redemptive.

Providing leadership, caring for people, teaching, preaching, and chairing meetings all seemed like acceptable and virtuous activities, having the potential for godliness and spirituality to be manifested. But fundraising? I knew it was in my job description, part of my duty, an obligation to be taken on, but I felt that it was in another category, almost a "dirty business," that was a necessary component of my work but lacking in nobility and substance. Our early conversations brought a sense of identification and kinship as we realized we shared this feeling of reluctance. We knew we were going to go to a particular destination, but we were not sure how to get there and why we wanted to go.

Friends and connections reinforced our shared reaction; sometimes they too perceived this part of our roles as unbecoming within our spiritual call. Unfortunately raising funds was something that leaders had to do, but if the organization was really true to its Christian roots and was living by faith, the business of raising funds would not occupy our time or activity. And, by implication, if we were true to our convictions and gifts we would not be absorbed with the raising of money. Being spiritually oriented and being a fundraiser were in opposition to one another. Surely there were better things to do with our time?

As I read books and went to seminars in the philanthropic arena, both Christian and secular, this distinction was further reinforced. Pragmatic, utilitarian, and how-to approaches dominated the landscape, and I had a deep sense that fundraising and spirituality were not on speaking terms and in fact had legalized their divorce. Fundraising, as a profession, seemed to operate in a very different way from how I understood the kingdom of Jesus Christ to be lived. It made me wonder if my reluctance to do this work was well founded.

I also detected various differing threads on the virtue of fundraising in the broader Christian world, all of which added to my confusion. Citing missionaries who "live by faith," some have nudged me to trust God and rely on him, not on raising money. So to mount a large campaign or build a significant endowment was seen as moving down a risk-reduction road to the point where we would "stop having faith in God to provide."

Some simply linked fundraising with need, so if there was a perceived need in the organization it was my task to simply tell people about the need and expect them to give. If people gave to that need, that was considered successful fundraising. The corollary was also true: if I did not raise funds for perceived needs, I had not been successful. In this context, raising money was really a "sales job" where sellers make a pitch to buyers and the good salespeople close the deal.

It is very strange to be engaged in work where the role itself is bathed in confusion. While accountants, homemakers, and schoolteachers receive their share of critique and evaluation, it would be highly unusual for a significant number of people to question the very virtue and validity of keeping accounts, hospitality, or teaching. But that is the world of the fundraiser, a world where there is not a well-understood and well-articulated summary of who fundraisers should be or what they should do. And then when spiritualized views of the pros and cons of the enterprise are factored in, it is no wonder that many of us doing this work experience reluctance. In fact, I wonder if this is why many who are involved in a ministry role that requires them to raise their own funds have a sense of disequilibrium. On the one hand, they embrace their service with understanding, passion, and enthusiasm; but on the other hand, with all the various messages on raising money, they naturally feel a disinclination toward that aspect of their responsibilities.

Joy

While the reactions and experiences of others have caused me pause, and at times have created angst, what has been most instructive is what has happened *to* me as I have engaged in fundraising. As I have reflected on my fundraising experiences and observations, I find that words like *conversion, transformation, spirituality, gospel, weakness,* and *kingdom of God* are now dominant in my thinking, and I realize that fundraising has changed *me.* I have had to recognize that the views of others were, in fact, my own views before embarking on this work, but I have learned something profound about myself and about God's work in the world through fundraising. It has ceased to be a "dirty business" and has become an arena where I have been given fresh glimpses into the gospel and God. In the end I have begun to wonder whether the critical success factor in fundraising is less about the amount of money raised and more about the *how* and the *why* of the process. Maybe only reluctance facilitates this kind of reflection and brings us to the place of joy.

My greatest experience of joy comes when I am in a transparent, vulnerable, and direct relationship with a donor where there is mutuality and reciprocity, and where we are aspiring together to determine what God is doing in the world and how we can help each other get in step with him. So many of my fundraising experiences have been of this nature, and that has cultivated joy. Put me in a relational context that lacks transparency, where communication is indirect, where there are power and control dynamics that negate mutuality, where personal concerns and challenges take over what God is doing, and where there does not appear to be any interest in getting in step with God, and I am lost. Not primarily mad, or angry, or frustrated. Lost. And there is no joy. Thankfully a much smaller number of donor connections were characterized by this mindset.

While I find it strange to admit to this, I have worked in clinics, agencies, hospitals, a private counseling practice, churches, parachurch organizations, and schools, but some of my greatest career joys have come in fundraising. I remember the first meeting I had with one donor couple who had been longtime supporters of the ministry when I arrived. In our first meeting we discussed the past and future of the organization and their commitment to it, but we also talked openly and honestly about our shared struggles in one area of life, and our mutual desire to follow God in the midst of overwhelming and consistent pain. Some might see such an interaction as negative or depressing, but in that initial interaction I experienced great joy. It was a merging of two human stories that started a foundation of friendship and relationship upon which the giving and receiving of money could be built. And when the husband of that couple told me that he was not going to retire but continue working so he could support the institution generously, I experienced the joy of watching someone making a major lifestyle commitment to support what God was doing.

I remember donor meetings where I went in discouraged or depressed, not expecting any money to come, and found the interaction to be life-giving and encouraging from a personal perspective.

Many donors with whom I have interacted have lost spouses, children, parents, marriages, or jobs, and the timing of our discussion about giving coincided with poignant moments of pain and angst. Not infrequently God seemed to have placed the same topic or concern on my mind as that of the donor, and our conversation went into spaces where co-pilgrimage was very evident.

While this was not a typical pattern, I did go into some donor meetings poorly prepared, lacking a spirit of gratitude and feeling pessimistic about the result, only to see God work in incredible ways. In fact, the three largest gifts I have ever been involved with came "in spite of me" not "because of me." Clearly God was at work, and in his grace and mercy he did not give me what I deserved, but clearly he was the one who provoked the giver to give generously. Joy oozes out of these experiences when you realize that God wants us to prepare, plan, and pray for donor engagement, but these human initiatives are not the sole prerequisite. When you see God at work in obvious ways and you are a very small part of the transaction, joy is inevitable.

I have both experienced and observed the joy that comes when organizational philanthropy is not the sole prerogative of the CEO or the fundraiser but is rooted in the prayerful and grateful attitude of a community of people. Fundraising teams that interact, pray, carry each other, rejoice, and agonize together create a foundation for work that is life-giving and stimulating. When the entire organization carries the emotional and spiritual weight of the work of philanthropy, there is the pure joy that comes because the people of God are actually functioning in a way that reflects their name.

Angst

Most enterprises can be summarized around four words—*why, who, how,* and *what.* Why am I doing what I am doing? Who am I doing it for? How am I doing what I am doing? What am

I doing? The greatest angst I have experienced and observed in philanthropy revolves around these four questions.

In the world of fundraising, secular or otherwise, there is a great stress on *what* fundraisers do, and much of that revolves around money raised. While that has its place, it seems to me there needs to be a greater stress on the *how*, the *who*, and the *why*. If fundraising is focused only on raising funds, then what makes so-called secular fundraising different from Christian fundraising? When someone goes online and raises funds for the publication of a book through crowdsourcing, how is that any different from a Christian missionary asking for donations so she can go to an AIDS-ravaged country in Africa to bring medical supplies? The *what* is the same. Funds are being raised for worthy causes, but if that is the end of the story and there is no consideration of *why*, *who*, and *how*, it is hard to assess the comparative virtue of the two campaigns. But so many fundraising drives are announced and assessed by the *what*—our target is $20 million or we raised $6 million—that we all become lulled into the belief that the *why*, the *who*, and the *how* are insignificant. I wonder if this has created an environment where we have no idea how the adjective *Christian* modifies the noun *fundraising*.

Over the years this tension has created angst for me as I have wanted to spend time, energy, passion, and interest on the central questions of *why* I am raising funds, *who* I am raising them for, and *how* I am doing it. But there is little time for that in this pragmatic, outcome-oriented culture where results are the sole measure of success because they are easily measured and observed. I have even wished that there was a lot more conversation about these issues with donors, but that runs the risk of looking like you are trying to spiritualize the interchange or manipulate their giving. I do know, however, that some donors have had experiences with fundraisers that have left a bad taste in their mouth. While many organizations are announcing "successful" campaigns, some of those who have contributed financially to its success would not use that word to describe their own involvement.

In my friend Peter I have found a conversation partner who keeps me honest and prevents me from aspiring solely to the *what,* to the exclusion of the other three. In our interactions I am constantly drawn to an integrated approach that reflects on the philanthropic enterprise not from the outside in—going from *what* to *how* to *who* to *why*—but rather from the inside out—going from *why* to *who* to *how* to *what.* I often come away from my time with Peter feeling like I need to think of fundraising as primarily a sphere preoccupied by the *why* and the *who,* with the result that the *how* is influenced and the *what* is a by-product.

Many fundraisers live in the pressure cooker of tight budgets, increased expenses, and lowered revenues, so there is an inherent corollary that pushes you toward the *"what* am I doing?" question. I was part of an educational institution where one of our supporters said he would give the school $300,000 if we gave his pastor an honorary doctorate. A similar situation occurred when a donor said they would pull their annual donation if we did not fire a particular professor. I have been in other circumstances where accepting a donation would have involved questionable ethics. In all these cases we recognized that we were in need of funds and we would lose financially by not acquiescing to the donor's terms. But it was not until we got into questions around *why* people give, *who* they are giving to, and *how* they give that we were able to deal with the financial angst that inevitably came by turning down the paid-for doctorate, dealing with the lack of funds resulting from the pay-for-firing donor, and ignoring the my-gift-has-some-baggage donor.

It is interesting that 2 Corinthians 8 and 9 pay little attention to the *what* of fundraising but focus on *why* we should give, *how* we should give, and *who* we are really giving to. What I have felt and observed is that this whole process is inverted in many Christian organizations. "We need to raise funds" becomes the primary answer to all philanthropic questions, and the values and virtues that need to undergird the *what* are left unattended. I even wonder whether our campaign targets or fundraising goals, often the product of careful planning and prognosticating, blur us to the reality of how the kingdom of God works. What would happen if our marketing brochures focused more on the *why, who,* and *how* and paid a little less attention to the *what*?

Angst about these questions, their place in the overall philanthropic arena, and the apparent lack of emphasis on them in the "industry" have created tension for me in raising funds.

4. What are your experiences with, and reflections on, the seven themes (integration, people, work, success, need, method, and money)?

Integration

One of the significant conversion experiences that I have had over the years in both observing and experiencing the world of philanthropy is the move away from a dualistic viewpoint where godliness is distinguished from money, to a perspective where God is over all and in all. Freed from the bondage of my own church history of two lists and two perspectives, I have had to learn an important lesson. Philanthropy, like preaching, the way I treat my wife, my approach to other relationships, my driving habits, my care for creation, and my reading of Scripture, all require an abiding faith in the triune God, a commitment to love him and love my neighbor, and a care for the entire creation that finds its source and origin in the Creator. Simple as it may seem, I often try to remind myself of these realities on the way to a donor meeting so I am in the right headspace when I arrive.

What has been hard about this conversion is that not all fundraisers, donors, and Christian organizations believe this to be the case, so I have often felt lonely in this kind of role, looking for conversation partners who will bring an integrated perspective to the discussion. I continue to run into Christians who are fundraising and who say they like sales, enjoy raising money, appreciate the buzz of closing a deal, but who do not seem to have a biblical or theological foundation for what they are doing. Some donors exhibit a pragmatic approach to giving, where their giving will be based on cash flow, personal interest or need, what might result for them with their gift, or whether they like the CEO. Organizations that designate themselves as Christian can easily fall into the dichotomy between their mission, ministry focus, and their fundraising arm. The former requires theological and biblical vision that is soaked in prayer and spiritual discernment, whereas the latter can turn into a way to bolster revenue for which any tool will do. When this kind of dichotomy is allowed to occur, the institution actually ceases to be Christian and shows an implicit avoidance of integration and a lack of understanding of how an organism works when it is infused with grace.

I wonder if philanthropic dualism has been facilitated by the need to turn fundraising into a formal field and profession. Those of us who raise funds, attend conferences, read books and blogs, and are members of various professional societies can easily come to believe that asking for money from others is an actual profession. Traditionally, professions are described in terms of three things: traits, that is, a common body of knowledge and skills; power, including assertion of power, social advantage, and earning capacity; and functionalism, in which we rely on professionals to do things we can no longer do for ourselves. So when I visit my dentist I see her as a professional because she has the particular skill and knowledge that would characterize all dentists; she has power and advantage over me because, even though the teeth are in my mouth, she understands them a lot better than I do; and it is far better for me to admit my amateur status, with no interest or expertise in dentistry, and secure the services of a professional.

This issue has come to the surface for me frequently when hiring fundraisers. Many of the applicants have formal membership in a fundraising association, they have skills and abilities that they claim help them raise funds, and they want to be in a role that pays them to be a professional. Over and over again, however, I find there is something else that I am looking for. There is an unmeasurable quality or characteristic or commitment that goes beyond "the profession." It is hard to put into words, but maybe it is less a desire to be a professional and more an interest in being an *amateur*, and an amateur in the sense of the original word as it was understood in Latin—doing it for love.

The professional side of fundraising definitely has its place, and I would not want my reflections here to be put into an either-or paradigm. We need fundraisers with skills and abilities, who see the profession as a viable one and find their vocational home in membership societies. But we also need people who love God and people, who are always asking where we fit into God's project—both the request and the response—who are willing to slow down in their activism and ask about kingdom priorities, who recognize that all giving has implications for creation and has the potential to transform the world. We need *Christian professionals* who understand that in doing the work of philanthropy they are *professing* something greater than themselves, their abilities, or their skills. They are *witnessing to* an identity that is rooted in the triune God, and to an approach to philanthropy that does not stand or fall on being a *professional* but on being an *amateur*. May God give us more *Christian amateurs* in the world of fundraising. I think that would address the loneliness many of us feel.

When you walk into many nonprofit organizations there are departments, functioning under terms like "development," "advancement," or "fundraising." Staffed by those who do the administrative work, they are often physically removed from the rest of the organization. While this reflects the reality of office assignments in an organization, it may also manifest a lack of integration that becomes very dangerous. I have seen too many organizations struggle with the perceptions, not of their constituencies or donors, but of colleagues whose workplace is in the same operation.

Observing those working in philanthropy, the core ministry people can easily bring a sense of "you are here to serve me," or "I am spending the money but you must bring it in," or "we are doing great work, so if the money is not coming in that is your fault." If they do not realize that fundraising is an integral part not just of the budget but also of the ministry itself, a line is created between "us" and "them," with little well-informed understanding going in either direction. When a Christian institution moves into a sphere where there is important, relevant, and spiritually oriented work in one part of the building, and pragmatic and utilitarian work in another part, a lack of integration has slipped in where not all are part of gospel work. Again, this lack of integration can create isolation and loneliness.

People

In all of the input on philanthropy from both the Christian and secular sectors I have not attended one talk, seminar, or conference, read one book or blog, or watched any online workshop that has had the title "Being nonrelational in fundraising," or "Raising funds without caring for others," or "How to raise funds without taking people seriously." Everyone believes that people are central in philanthropy, but in fundraising, like many other endeavors, it is easy to forget the centrality of people, to move into a goal-setting pragmatic trajectory, to overvalue the financial aspect of the transaction and use relationality as a means to an end. In my experience this value drift has occurred, not when I stop prizing the nebulous concept of "people," but when I fail to understand the uniqueness of each "person."

I have learned, for instance, that it is beneficial to ask each potential donor how they like to talk about money, what preferences they have in terms of institutional connection and communication, how they like to be treated when a request is put in front of them, and what are their particular philanthropic interests. Some people like to speak about financial matters openly and honestly, want extensive communication from the organization, want their decision about giving to be an ongoing dialogue with you the fundraiser, and have specific interests and passions. Others would prefer to avoid the subject of money even though it is a fundraising visit, do not want to be on mailing lists, make it very clear that they will initiate and respond to the invitation on their timeline, and are not open about the nature of their passions. Being committed to people cannot mean approaching everyone the same way, but requires a respect for individuality and uniqueness.

Because I have done a lot of fundraising cross-culturally, I have become aware that understanding the link between ethnicity, money, and fundraising requires a particular kind of sensitivity and wisdom. In China, for instance, I have come to understand that love and respect are demonstrated through food, so I will be eating a lot of meals, with multiple courses, and the food will be ordered for me. Because it is a context where family, heritage, and history matter, I have learned that talking to potential donors about their family, children, and parents is not only polite but appropriate and culturally sensitive. Although I do not come from a shame-based culture, I now recognize that people raised in traditional Chinese culture construct their world with hierarchy and roles so that those who are higher up in status should not be shamed by those who are lower down. Even if I would ask Chinese donors for some negative feedback, it would be hard for them to give it because as a Caucasian male in a position of authority I might be shamed as a result. Similarly, face-saving is a key component of this culture, so being direct or frank would be seen as overbearing and controlling, causing the recipient to lose face and back away from the relationship. While authenticity, vulnerability, and transparency are valued in many parts of Western culture, such a posture in a relationship with a Chinese person is culturally insensitive and will get in the way of an appropriate discussion of giving.

While these are interesting cultural variables, they are challenging for the fundraiser. Does an inability to get a meeting set up indicate that the Chinese donor is unavailable, unwilling, or not interested at all? Might you have done something inappropriate in a previous meeting that has soured the relationship with the donor or caused them to lose face? Does the fact that no donation has come through in spite of multiple meetings and invitations indicate a "no," or a "maybe eventually if you keep meeting with me"? These questions are not confined to Western or Eastern cultures; they also apply within North America and between North America and Europe, even though each has its cultural distinctives. Within the emerging field of African philanthropy, the dynamics are different again. While directness about many things, including money, characterizes much of the United States, Canadians are slightly more reticent in this area and in that sense are more like Europeans, who often react quite negatively to the boldness of American philanthropy. Fundraisers who want to be sensitive to people but work cross-culturally need to ensure that they understand these variables through study and attentive engagement with those from other cultures.

People are very different, and there are no easy rules for discerning why they want to meet with fundraisers and the nature of their core motivation. Not infrequently, fundraisers find that the donors who give the most money are often the most reluctant to meet and the least demanding. "You have other people to meet with," we are told. "Spend time with them and don't worry about me. I love your organization and will continue giving." At the other extreme, some so-called fundraising conversations are not about the giving of money; instead, they are a way for the potential donor to share opinions, information, even directives, and the interaction becomes a context for that to happen. The fundraiser becomes a conduit to the organization rather than someone who is seeking for funds on its behalf. Many people of wealth live somewhat isolated lives and do not have many intimate friends. In multiple ways their money can become a barrier protecting them from community and relationship. Meeting with fundraisers can become a legitimized form of connecting and prove to be less about giving money and more about experiencing friendship.

For me, discerning the motivation of philanthropists, and then deciding how to respond, has been one of the more challenging aspects of paying attention to people in fundraising. How long does one meet with a potential donor before concluding that their motivation is not about giving funds? Do you continue to meet to honor other motivations or is that irresponsible in the light of your job expectations? How do you interpret the "cannot meet you right now" or "let's get together next month" or "sorry, I have to cancel our meeting," when you have already set up your schedule, booked your flight, and secured accommodation? What is the relationship between patience, perseverance, and pestering? Do donor connections come to an end at the fundraiser's initiative, or that of the donor, or is it some combination? Having a person-centered approach to philanthropy does not eliminate these nagging questions, which require wisdom and prayer.

Websites, blogs, social media, crowdfunding, databases, search engines, and staffing support have all contributed to a philanthropic industry that has more accessibility to people than ever before. While it would be naïve to dismiss all technological and administrative supports as suspect, it is equally dangerous to move fundraising out of face-to-face interaction completely and rely on these "advances." It seems to me that keeping persons in focus allows us to resist the impersonality of an approach to fundraising where everything is done technologically and administratively.

How can we keep persons in focus? We are keeping persons in focus when "smaller donors" are called and thanked by the executive director. When the administrative staff does not do their work just on screens, but on the phone and in person. When donors receive personal letters, even handwritten, rather than form letters that are clearly not sent by people. When initial gifts to an organization are acknowledged carefully and specifically, not generically and impersonally. When administrative staff are included in team meetings and prayer collectives and they sense that they are just as much a part of the request as those "on the road." When letters are signed by a real person with a real pen. When all donors are phoned, even if it is just leaving a message, and thanked within twenty-four hours of the reception of the gift. When gifts are celebrated communally, reflecting a spirit of gratitude and appreciation. All of these little things, and many more, keep us focused on persons, reminding us of our essence as both fundraisers and donors, equally created in the image of God.

Work

One of the biggest challenges for me as a fundraiser has been a clear and appropriate understanding of the nature of my work. I am moved that the apostle Paul understands his work as a pastor, teacher, evangelist, and fundraiser as part of his relationship with Christ and that his performance in these various roles is tied to this core identity. And it is noticeable that he sees all his work as essentially God's work and he is simply a participant. I have found it hard to stay settled in that space and easier to live out of other, unhealthy mindsets.

I remember going to lunch with a donor I did not know very well. It came in the midst of a busy season, with many other appointments and commitments, and I did not go into the meeting well prepared, spiritually ready, or emotionally in tune. All fundraisers know that experience. The meeting has been set, you know you need to be there, obligation trumps all else, and you show up. I had offered up a brief prayer along the lines of "God help me," but my expectation of anything happening at all was quite low, my belief that I could do anything to make something happen was even lower, and while I knew God could do something, my implicit theology was lacking in hope. That lunch meeting turned into four hours of warm engagement and surprising connection, and after a few more similar meetings it turned into a gift of $3.3 million. The lesson? God's work is not dependent on our preparedness or our effort.

I know of another situation where an executive director of a good-sized nonprofit spent an inordinate amount of time, prayer, preparation, and planning to secure a very large gift from an individual who expressed a definite interest in making the gift. Multiple meetings took place over a few years, and each one ended on a positive note, leading the executive director to assume that a gift would come in due time. At each stage of the process the attitude of the executive director remained rooted in God's provision and his work both in the life of the organization and in the life of the donor. In the end the donor indicated via a brief email that they would not be giving the gift. The lesson? God's work is not dependent on our effort.

Nevertheless, I have to confess that the absence of a linear relationship between my fundraising work and its financial outcome has been extremely frustrating. I would like to think that human effort and energy would guarantee a particular result, especially when most Christian fundraisers are seeking to position their work based on their identity in Christ. However, whether the executive director works extremely hard and does not see an obvious result, or employs minimal human effort and sees an amazing outcome, one is left with the feeling that God really is in control and we as fundraisers need to carry our work lightly since it is in

God's hands. For me, it has meant moving out of an industrial or manufacturing image where I can make something and be in control of that process, into more of an agricultural image where I can plant seed with diligence and thoroughness but recognize that the growth and the harvest are beyond my control.

For me, the best test of how I understand my work as a fundraiser is the emotional spirit that I bring to it. In one of my fundraising roles I was in a context where the organization was struggling financially. I was being criticized by some people for not having a big enough vision to bring in significant funds, and as a consequence I began to slip into the mode of a functional atheist. I started believing that income from philanthropy was completely my responsibility and that if I worked harder, put in more time, and visited more donors I could produce the desired result. My pace became frantic, my schedule nonsensical, and I met donors endlessly for a number of months. The dominant emotions were fear and panic, and the gentleness and tranquility of the Holy Spirit were noticeably absent. My body and spirit took a beating and the financial results were meager. Through pain I had to learn again about the nature of the work for the Christian fundraiser. God's work is not dependent on our effort.

Although 1 Kings 18 has absolutely nothing to do with philanthropy, I have found it incredibly helpful in understanding my relationship to God's work. On Mount Carmel a major spiritual battle occurs as Elijah challenges God's enemies to see who can bring fire down from heaven on humanly constructed altars. The prophets of Baal call on him from morning until noon, dance around the altar, shout loudly, slash themselves with swords and spears until blood flows, and behave in a frantic manner. The result? "But there was no response; no one answered" (v. 29). Elijah, in contrast, quietly sets up his altar, douses it with water three times to make it even more difficult for fire to consume it, steps back, and prays. The result? "Then the fire of the Lord fell and burned up the sacrifice, the wood, the stones and the soil, and also licked up the water in the trench" (v. 38). If my work as a fund-raiser is rooted in my identity in Christ, led by the Holy Spirit and an expression of worship to the Father, then I do all my activity with a recognition that he is in charge, he is accomplishing what he wants to achieve with his own standards for faithfulness, and I do not need to live frantically. I fear too many of us fundraisers who call ourselves Christians are spending too much time slashing ourselves with swords and spears. And then there is that niggling memory of the times we have prayed and expected God to do his work and the altar was not consumed.

Remembering the backdrop of 2 Corinthians 8 and 9, I have experienced and observed situations where fundraising is as basic as we are trying to get money in because we need it. Eyes are not focused up on something bigger and wider; our actions are pragmatic and simplistic. Like the apostle in his particular situation, I yearn to see more Christian organizations invite potential donors to give because it is *gospel work*. Give because it is going to accomplish more significant purposes. Give because there is more going on than meets the eye. Give because money is one means by which we accomplish God's purposes in the world.

Success

In trying to understand the nature of fundraising work on a day-by-day basis, I have been forced to come to grips with success and failure. In one of my fundraising roles I traveled a lot and would often return to the office to hear the question "How did it go?" The response "I don't know" would not bring me credibility or trust, but it was often what I was thinking. How did it go? I had a lot of meetings, spoke at quite a number of events, presented the mission and needs of the institution in the most compelling way I knew how, and asked a lot of people to consider giving a gift. Some people said they would consider giving, others said they could not do anything right now, one wrote a check, a few were critical of the institution and its current direction, some asked me to come back and talk more about a particular project, and some showed no interest at all. On top of that one of my flights got canceled, there was a family emergency while I was away, and I picked up a bad cold on the plane; but I enjoyed the people I met, I had one really good conversation about vocational direction with someone who was moving into a new career, and the worship in the church where I preached was outstanding.

Pastors, preachers, teachers, evangelists, and cross-cultural workers all go through the same experience when it comes to the evaluation of ministry. What is a successful pastor? Preacher? Teacher? Evangelist? Is the mission worker who serves cross-culturally for twenty years considered a success? Does he need to engage in a certain amount of work for social justice to be successful? Is a particular number of conversions required? When do we determine a pastor has been a failure? What does she need to do wrong, or not do right, in order to reach that standard? If Christian fundraising is part of kingdom work, and it is being done in a kingdom way, then only kingdom values can be used to ascertain true success and failure. I have a lot to learn in understanding what this means, and I want to keep growing in this area.

I remember talking to a fundraising department head about her experience in a board meeting. She presented her numbers for the fiscal year and during the question period was asked, "How many people do you have in your department?" After she gave the answer, one member responded with, "I know an organization that has half that number on their development team and they raise a lot more money." That led to a difficult interaction in which the department head was forced to account for the lack of funds raised. She left the meeting feeling like a failure, wondering if her staff would be cut because they were seen as "not performing."

Such a discussion raises questions about who is measuring and by what criteria and whether the way we raise funds even matters. Perhaps it would be worthwhile for boards and senior management to examine how they make their fundraisers accountable and whether this way is aligned with the wider Christian thinking that guides the organization. We do need to be accountable in our fundraising work, but we need to understand the complexity of how this is done.

In my experience, multiple measurement devices are needed if we are going to assess fundraising well, and this will involve both tangible and nontangible outcomes. Assuming the presence of high-quality staff and software systems, accountability is relatively easily achieved in the tangible outcome category. Under the fundraiser rubric, the number of personal meetings / phone calls / online messages is a simple way to determine if the fundraiser is actually connecting with donors. Normally a full-time fundraiser will have twelve to fifteen face-to-face meetings per month with an active portfolio of 125 to 150 donors, assuming they are doing careful preparation and follow-up as part of those visits. Under the gifts rubric it is possible to see whether a gift is restricted by the donor in how it is used or if it is unrestricted. How many in-kind gifts are being donated where actual physical items are given in exchange for a tax receipt? Are gifts being given for the annual fund, special-purpose funds, campaign, or endowment? To get even more technical, in some donor rubrics people's responses can be designated as "lybunt" (last year but unfortunately not this) or "sybunt" (some year but unfortunately not this). Under a process rubric, organizations can document the number of inquiry letters and requests for proposals from individuals or foundations, and in some cases can ascertain where donors or organizations are in education, engagement, empathy, and enlightenment, four terms that comprise what is called "moves management" in philanthropy-speak.

One small example of the importance of understanding such metrics is in the area of what is known as donor retention. I have observed that organizations can get frustrated with their fundraising department because the annual fund is not growing. While a failure to grow can usually be traced to a multiplicity of variables, there are hard facts in retention research that show the median retention rate of donors, across the fundraising world, is 43 percent. That means only 43 percent of individuals who gave to organizations last year will give this year. Phrased another way, this means the average organization needs to gain 57 percent new donors every year in order to maintain the number of contributing donors. Retention of new donors runs anywhere from 23 to 28 percent, meaning that over 70 percent of donors make an initial gift and do not return. If the scale of the work can yield sufficient data to show boards or senior management significant trends, they need to bring a level of sophistication to the task of measuring their fundraisers' success or failure, and not simply glance superficially at a single number in a report.

In the nontangible area, three facets of fundraising "success" have struck me as being crucial: time frame, grace, and spiritual benefit. When those of us who raise funds are doing our work, it happens at a particular point in time, but it has a historical context and an unknown future. I have had the experience of obtaining a gift for an organization but it was my predecessor who actually laid the groundwork in previous meetings. In some cases particular donors contributed more than they had in the past, and sometimes I was able to develop a relationship with a donor where my predecessor was unable to do so. In all these cases, his so-called failure turned into my apparent success.

But linking the present with the past is only half the story. People of faith who do their work with faithfulness recognize that all that is done in the present is framed in the context of the future, not just the future in my life but the final future toward which all things are moving. It may be that a month or a year from now I will see the results of my work, but it may also be that I will see no gift—with the attendant assessment of "failure." Equally, it may happen that my successor will visit that same person and my watering will result in him seeing a plant, giving him the "success" designation. Both I and my successor will hear the ultimate and final judgment of all things done in the body and find out that not only were our designations of "success" and "failure" inaccurate, but the metrics themselves completely missed the ultimate point, at least from God's perspective.

The second nontangible measurement revolves around grace and the natural streams that flow out of that river—gift, generosity, and gratitude. When donors experience these realities and give with generosity, and their donation is received as gift, gratitude flows to God from the recipient and from the donor. I remember hearing from a small group of donors who had given almost half a million dollars to some employees in a Christian institution. Few of the employees acknowledged the gift at all, and the donors had the sense that their generosity had hardly been appreciated. They were not giving in order to get a thank you; they gave because of their understanding of grace, gift, and generosity, and they were surprised when it was not reciprocated. When those donors were asked at a later date to give another large gift to benefit those same employees, they refused because of a fear that entitlement had replaced gratitude. In this case the fundraising was a failure, not because a gift was not secured but because the spirit in which it was received lacked a true understanding of the gospel. While these intangibles might be hard to measure by a board, senior management, or the fundraisers themselves, all fundraising needs to be bathed in grace, gift, gratitude, and generosity in order to be deemed a "success."

The final nontangible is the spiritual benefit to the donor, a point that Paul emphasizes extensively in 2 Corinthians 8 and 9. Over and over again I have run into people who have willingly and enthusiastically parted with their money in order to bless others. In the process they themselves have received more blessing, have had a deeper understanding of God's grace, have been stimulated to give generously on other occasions, and have been thankful to God. While the organization might have benefited from the gift, the deeper consequence is that the philanthropists learned that it is more blessed to give than to receive. Maybe more of our assessments, judgments, and conclusions on how well our fundraising drive went need to be refocused to ask about our donors, their spiritual recalibration, and the benefits they derived from giving. Maybe we also need to take a fresh look at the distinction between *charity*, the historic practice where donors gave to express gratitude and to exercise the spiritual discipline of generosity, and the more contemporary work of *philanthropy*, where money is given to achieve improvement in the world. Does the biblical record distinguish between these two, or should all giving reflect the best of charity and philanthropy?

It is relatively easy to make pronouncements about who and what is successful and what constitutes failure, and even easier if we value the tangible and seen and ignore the intangible and unseen. While welcoming examination and critique of our plans and methods, those of us who work as fundraisers need to resist such superficial assessments and wait patiently and with expectation to hear a more holistic judgment—and not least from the Judge of all.

Need

While I believe the distinction between need and call is an important one biblically and theologically, I have found it really challenging to bring that perspective to the daily work of fundraising. After all, is that not what philanthropy is about? Donors with money are matched with organizations and individuals with needs. Most of us who board the fundraising train end up at that destination, but I wonder if there is another destination or maybe a different train. And I also wonder whether a fresh look at this subject might not benefit donors.

Having been involved with particular donors for a significant period of time, I have been struck by how many of them want to talk about "donor fatigue," a pithy description of the weariness they are experiencing with the overwhelming demands in the philanthropic arena. The core of the problem is that those of us who raise funds are presenting so many needs that we are drowning people in requests. Statistics abound on the number of organizations coming on-stream with more and more needs, so we have to come to terms with the fact that donor fatigue is probably not going to decrease but increase. As technology increasingly allows us to "contact personally" a greater number of people, so the opportunities for those with needs to reach those with means to help expands exponentially.

I wonder what would happen if we stopped trying to expand our donor base, encouraging more people to give, and inviting those who give to do more, and tried instead to take the focus off our needs and put it more on the spiritual benefit to the donor and the bigger call of what God is doing in the world. What if we knew our donors so well that we could work with them to ascertain what God is doing in their lives, how they are being called to give, and how our organization might fit into that call? Because we are so institution-specific in fundraising, that might mean we would "lose" a donor to another organization, but with a kingdom mindset is that such a bad thing? What if we asked bigger questions about global and creation issues and worked with donors to listen to God's perspective? Might that mean that our particular institutional "need" seems insignificant, even unimportant, as we realize that there are bigger issues at stake than meeting some need that we have judged of high value? My reading of 2 Corinthians 8 and 9 is that Paul is more concerned about the relationship between Jews and Gentiles than he is about the poverty of the Jewish believers, not that the latter is insignificant, but the former is foundational.

My interaction with donors over the years has led me into many conversations about the viability and appropriateness of our "needs." I would present the institutional perspective and my viewpoint on our needs, and sometimes what I would get in return was not money but an astute analysis of our need. A lot of my fundraising work has been based in Toronto and Vancouver, the two most expensive cities in Canada. Staff in many parachurch institutions and churches in these two locations struggle with the cost of living and the affordability of housing, and from our internal perspective we see these things as needs. In presenting this challenge to donors I have described the distance employees have to travel and the impact this has not just on the individual but on institutional well-being and mission. For me, this was a need that could be addressed by increasing salaries or providing affordable housing. One donor said he would donate money to buy a bus so the employees could commute to and from work together and this would build collegiality and cut costs. Another donor gave me a grid on salaries in Canada that showed our employees as among the better paid, so more money for this group was not an option. Someone else indicated that the institution should move to a location where people could afford to live. And one lunch meeting left me with the distinct feeling, "This is a first-world problem in a large urban center—live with it."

When I return from these kinds of interactions I am often in a quandary. The institution and the staff who comprise it are actually experiencing need, the donors are not demonstrating empathy to the need but an evaluation of it, and as the fundraiser I am left to arbitrate between the two. It has made me reflect on the danger of needy communities making internal judgments without the full involvement of the donor community.

But how can that be done? Do we bring all our donors together and ask their opinions? Viability studies are often utilized for this; a third party interviews donors to determine their level of interest in a particular project and their potential financial capacity in giving to it, but often the project has been predetermined by the institution. While these have their place, I wonder whether we as Christian fundraisers can do more to link with our donors in heart and prayer before we even consider a link with the wallet. It sounds administratively cumbersome and maybe a little utopian, but would there be any way that we could frame God's will as a communal process where an entire constituency prayed and discerned, listened to the Father's call, and moved together as one? Would institutions be willing to reconceptualize donors as members of the body and allow those donors to be full participants in watching for the God sightings, promptings, and opportunities that flow out of that attentiveness? Rather than starting with need, we would be engaging in a spiritual process that has value in and of itself; we would be concerned for the spiritual benefits that donors would receive by their giving; and our energies would not focus on getting "supporters to give," but rather the influx of money would be a natural by-product of being a "member of the body." Thus the unity of the church of Jesus Christ would be expressed.

I remember having an evening meeting where I brought together a dozen longstanding supporters of our institution to present them with a potential vision for the future before it was announced publicly, asking them not only for their opinions but also for their prayer. They were hand-selected because they had invested considerable time, talent, and finances over the years and it seemed wise to allow them to express their critique of an envisioned future and commit it to God along with our community. It was a risky meeting, as requesting feedback is often perceived as synonymous with completely handing over responsibility and authority, but it was received as respectful and hospitable, and it provided me with nuances and prayer partners that I would not have had if the institution had proceeded alone.

I worry for church and parachurch organizations who have locked into the "I have a need—you have money" paradigm. Just as infants, who assume life is about their needs being met, have to grow up and realize "the other" is there for relationship, community, and interdependence and not merely as the answer to all their screaming, so too Christian communities need to mature. Organizations that stay in an autonomous, need-centered posture disconnected from the so-called "outside" constituency will eventually find themselves talking to themselves, resenting the lack of interest from donors, and struggling financially.

Method

I talked earlier about fundraising bringing me feelings of reluctance, joy, and angst. These emotions, like any experience of feeling, drive each of us to engage in particular aspirations and behaviors. For me, my angst had led me into a way of thinking that was focused exclusively on method and means. In the desire to raise lots of money and to make the organization financially strong, I have found it easy to focus on ways and means to make that happen. Although my natural propensity takes me away from "how-to's" and superficial efficiency schemes, fundraising angst has produced some strange directions. "If I just did . . . then . . ." became an operative paradigm, and I believed that the chaos in my gut would be resolved by finding foolproof methods. This in spite of the fact that I had learned in doing counseling and in my own experience that many people raised in emotional chaos will resort to controlling, orderly ways of dealing with the world, stemming from the illusion that this will lessen their angst.

When our method becomes its own solution, fundraisers get into trouble, and I am painfully aware of that in my own life. If the gospel is to permeate my philanthropic world, method will be a piece of my work, but it must be infused with a recognition that this is ultimately God's work, and therefore any belief that painstaking attention to my "how-to's" will ease my discomfort is a slow road to nowhere. I have had to learn that my inner struggles are an invitation to recalibrate and learn again that human effort is a feeble substitute for God's action. I have found it incredibly helpful to be aware of my natural tendency to go from angst to wanting a superb method; I then realize that my angst can drive me to experience my own helplessness and embrace the need to call on the triune God. Such a process is ongoing and often painful.

You could argue that such an approach is hardly a method, but I am beginning to wonder if the "how-to" nature of contemporary culture has squeezed us into a way of viewing things whereby we really do believe that with the right approach we can make anything happen. And such a mindset is not confined to fundraising. Techniques and tried-and-true methods guaranteed to improve various aspects of church life and church growth are on offer everywhere. But the more I have realized that much of kingdom work *happens*, the more I have had to realize that the God who provided manna in the wilderness is the same God who is working with the contemporary fundraiser, that the Holy Spirit who birthed the church after the resurrection of Jesus Christ is the same Holy Spirit who is at work in the organization, the fundraiser, and the philanthropist. It may not play well in some circles, but more and more I am experiencing the work of fundraising as watching for Divine appointments and being ready for God sightings.

This argument could lead some organizations to fire their database manager and online gifts person and rework their entire administration. But having worked with high-quality philanthropic administrators who have the right orientation, I know there is a way for people in these essential roles to carry out methodological tasks with gospel expectancy rather than method as solution. The presence of the right tone, a godly spirit, genuine prayer, respectful relationality, and healthy conflict resolution all require Christ-centeredness. As Paul demonstrated in 2 Corinthians, thoughtfulness and care in carrying out administrative tasks are a gift of the Spirit and in no way antithetical to being a Christian. It amazes me how many Christian organizations fail to express personal gratitude for a gift, mess up tax receipts, cannot handle address changes, almost never talk about the biblical and theological components of philanthropy, or lose all relationality because they are driven exclusively by technology. Christian fundraising requires a higher standard.

Because Paul's emphasis in 2 Corinthians 9:7 is on each person deciding about her gift in her heart and doing this service cheerfully, and by implication not doing it "reluctantly or under compulsion," an ongoing methodological focus on motive and intent has been important for me. A large part of fundraising is about persuasive communication, and it is persuasive because we have an intent. We are trying to influence someone's beliefs, attitudes, behavior, mindset, and convictions, with the hope that a gift will ensue. If we deceive people in our presentation of the case, imprint our envelopes with crisis-oriented messages that do not reflect a genuine emergency, send email messages that do not tell the whole story of the institutional request, employ spokespeople who do not have a genuine, well-established interest in our organization, or feign friendliness, we are using methods that are manipulative or deceptive. In essence we are endeavoring to control and are moving from persuasive communication to manipulation.

Being aware of oneself and the potential strain of wanting to be successful, while simultaneously attending to God and trusting in his power and provision, and being sensitive to the potential funders and their passions and capacity to choose—this may be the most important "method" in Christian fundraising. Giving time, energy, interest, and discernment *in* to oneself, *up* to God, and *out* to the donor is a costly sacrifice and much less efficient than "six steps to successful fundraising" or "learn how to fundraise in seven minutes."

Money

I have found it helpful to have a clear template on money when I do fundraising so that I can put it in proper perspective at a personal level and not slip into the mindset that Christian fundraising is solely about funds. As a result, issues around identity, disconnection, and worship occupy a lot of my attention and inform my understanding of fundraising. In our personal lives, Bev and I have learned through success and failure that if our *being* is bathed in God's goodness and beneficence, we carry money lightly and find it easier to give it to others so they are blessed. We have also learned that having our identities rooted in having, acquiring, and possessing leads to consuming, coveting, and craving, with the result that we want to keep our money for ourselves. Reinforced by Western secular culture where "pride of ownership" and unbridled consumerism are givens, we have found it easy to slip into an identity wrapped up in money.

These two paths, leading out of *being* or *having*, are all about where we find our core and foundation, and they naturally result in *doing*. If my *being* finds its home in God, my *doing* will be centered on a life of giving because I am absorbed by grace, gift, and gratitude. In contrast, if *having* is my dominant posture, giving will not be at the core of my *doing*, but I will find it easy to consume, covet, and crave, so will tend to keep my money in order to fulfill these objectives. Since I was a little boy I have been struck by Jesus's explanation in Luke 12:15 as to why greed is a problem—"life does not consist in an abundance of possessions." Translation? If you think life in all its fullness is about *having* and not *being*, you have missed the point.

A disconnection between money and spiritual values eventually moves us as individuals and as a culture to a place where money becomes disconnected from its instrumental value, as a means to purchase goods and services, to a place where money becomes an end itself. Simply making and having money with the financial independence that ensues moves us to a place where the utilitarian capacity of money to buy is no longer dominant. If money becomes our ultimate goal, it emerges as an idol. However, the evolution of money from instrument to idol is apparent not just in the worlds of the wealthy; it can also afflict those with little money. If we are sold a message that having money bestows an ultimate value on us, we can easily strive to gain more and more or at least to work hard to be seen as people with money. I suspect a lot of indebtedness, excessive loans, high mortgages, and maxed-out lines of credit can be traced back to a disconnect between money and spirituality, to treating money as idol not instrument, or to a desire to give the impression that because we have money we have status and significance.

When these issues of identity and disconnection are clarified by the Holy Spirit, "philanthropy as worship" becomes possible. It is why Paul in Philippians 4:18 can describe the financial gift from the church in a threefold way: as "a fragrant offering, an acceptable sacrifice, pleasing to God." I have found my own giving is deeply impacted when I move away from cultural messages about money and embrace this powerful triad. When I prepare for donor meetings, it is helpful to know that I am moving into the arena of worship and not simply engaging in a financial transaction. My primary understanding of philanthropists is not tied to their monetary capacity but to their relationship with the triune God and his work in their lives. It is amazing how a fundraiser's anxieties and fears can be silenced when together we realize that we are in a realm that is about bringing pleasure to God, offering him something that is acceptable.

When a pastor prepares a Sunday morning sermon he or she is embarking on an enterprise that is about connecting the lives of people with God himself. A worship leader who selects Scripture, prayers, and music is not engaging in a solo performance but is developing a liturgy that will guide the participants into the very life of God. The evangelist, youth pastor, church administrator, and all others who have particular roles in the body of Christ are doing the same thing in their desire to connect, guide, and lead people into greater intimacy with the Father, Son, and Holy Spirit. Fundraising is, or should be, no different. In many ways the work of philanthropy can see the fundraiser as liturgist, preparing, planning, and leading worship with all the attendant attitudes of prayerfulness and spiritual sensitivity that would be demanded from anyone who is seeking to bring the people of God into communion with their Creator and Redeemer.

Conceptualizing myself as a liturgist in the work of fundraising has led me to be cautious with people who engage in impression management and not worship when it comes to money, presenting themselves as potential donors simply because they want to be seen as "in" or "part of" an organization or a relationship. I now pay more attention to how people made their money to help facilitate a God consciousness and a true worship sensibility. I am less interested in donors who have lost the link between worship and wealth and use their giving or lack of giving as some sort of leverage, exertion of power, or lack of endorsement of people or organizations. I have come to realize that the "best" donors are not necessarily those with high financial capacity, but those who recognize that philanthropy has the ability to transform individuals, organizations, and the planet and ultimately be a form of worship of God. Finally, I want to use philanthropic terminology that accurately reflects reality under the canopy of God's sovereignty and not be afraid to talk about worship, sacrifice, and offering as they apply to the world of philanthropy.

CHAPTER 12

A Fundraiser's Prayer

Good Father,

Giver of every good and perfect gift,
Lord of a universe characterized by abundance
     and not scarcity,

Grant us the capacity to do all our fundraising
as we would all other aspects of the life
     that reflects Christ.

Grant us the insight to see all donors as image bearers
who have the privilege of worshiping you
     through their giving.

Grant us the grace to do our work with diligence,
all the while recognizing that your work is not
     dependent on our efforts.

Grant us the vision to allow gift, grace, and gratitude
to invite us into joyful service.

A Fundraiser's Prayer

Grant us the faith to see that the benefit to the donor
and the strengthening of your body are foundational
    to all our activities.

Grant us the courage to be prayerfully attentive
    to your work in the world
so that our fundraising methods flow from that source.

Grant us the conviction that the raising of funds
    is not an end in itself
but an outcome of a life immersed in the gospel.

We offer these our prayers in the name of the one
    who was rich,
yet for our sakes became poor, the indescribable gift,
    Jesus Christ.

Amen.

Notes

1. See Belden C. Lane's fascinating account of this in *Ravished by Beauty: The Surprising Legacy of Reformation Theology* (Oxford: Oxford University Press, 2011).

2. Makoto Fujimura, *On Becoming Generative: An Introduction to Culture Care* (New York: Fujimura Institute, 2013), 2.

3. Personal letter, 19 November 1982.

4. The story of A Rocha is found in Peter Harris, Susan Rubira, and John Stott, *Under the Bright Wings* (Vancouver: Regent College Publishing, 2000).

5. Harris, Rubira, and Stott, *Under the Bright Wings*, 72-73.

6. See for example Russell D. Moore, "Heaven and Nature Sing: How Evangelical Theology Can Inform the Task of Environmental Protection (and Vice Versa)," *Journal of Evangelical Theological Studies* 57, no. 3 (2014): 571-88.

7. Dave Bookless, *God Doesn't Do Waste* (Downers Grove, IL: IVP, 2010); Leah Kostamo, *Planted* (Eugene, OR: Cascade, 2013); Chris Naylor, *Postcards from the Middle East* (Oxford: Lion Hudson, 2015).

8. Ellen Davis, *Proverbs, Ecclesiastes and the Song of Songs* (Louisville: Westminster John Knox, 2000), 26-27.

9. Ellen Davis, *Scripture, Culture and Agriculture* (Cambridge: Cambridge University Press, 2009).

10. Davis, *Scripture, Culture and Agriculture*, 22.